THE TEXAS BUCKET LIST GUIDE BOOK

110+ Amazing Adventures & Places to Explore to Make Your Travel Dreams Come True!

Primeveler Publishing

Legal & Disclaimer © 2023

The information contained in this book and its contents is not meant to replace the need for independent medical, financial, legal or other professional advice or services, as may be required. The content and information in this book has been provided for educational and entertainment purposes only.

The content and information contained in this book has been compiled from sources deemed reliable, and it is accurate to the best of the Author's knowledge, information and belief. However, the Author cannot guarantee its accuracy and validity and cannot be held liable for any errors and/or omissions. Further, changes are periodically made to this book as and when needed. Where appropriate and/or necessary, you must consult a professional (including but not limited to your doctor, attorney, financial advisor or such other professional advisor) before using any of the suggested remedies, techniques, or information in this book.

Upon using the contents and information contained in this book, you agree to hold harmless the Author from and against any damages, costs, and expenses, including any legal fees potentially resulting from the application of any of the information provided by this book. This disclaimer applies to any loss, damages or injury caused by the use and application, whether directly or indirectly, of any advice or information presented, whether for breach of contract, tort, negligence, personal injury, criminal intent, or under any other cause of action.

You agree to accept all risks of using the information presented inside this book.

You agree that by continuing to read this book, where appropriate and/or necessary, you shall consult a professional (including but not limited to your doctor, attorney, or financial advisor or such other advisor as needed) before using any of the suggested remedies, techniques, or information in this book.

Copyright note: 2023

This book is intended for educational and informational purposes only. No express or implied guarantee is made between you and the publisher in regards to the information provided within this publication, nor is any representation that the information will be used as a replacement for professional advice rendered by a qualified therapist/professional. The publisher makes no representations or warranties with respect to the accuracy or completeness of the contents of this work and specifically disclaims any implied warranties of merchantability or fitness for a particular purpose.

The information contained herein is stated to be truthful and consistent, as either an attribute of the publisher or organization describing itself. Under no circumstances will any legal liability or blame be held against the publisher for any reparability, damages, or monetary loss due to the information herein. As we strive to give you all the information as conveniently and enjoyable as possible. We also appreciate your feedback on how to improve our efforts. 2023 is the year of thought, innovation and creativity.

TABLE OF CONTENTS

INTRODUCTION 1
ABOUT TEXAS 2
   Climate and Landscape 3
   The Map of Texas 4
HOW TO USE THIS GUIDE 5

AMARILLO
   1. Cadillac Ranch 6
   2. Amarillo Botanical Garden 8
   3. Palo Duro Canyon State Park 9
   4. Texas Air & Space Museum 10

ARLINGTON
   5. Six Flags Over Texas 11
   6. Arlington Museum of Art 13

AUSTIN
   7. McKinney Falls State Park 14
   8. Bullock Texas State History Museum 15
   9. Texas Capitol 16
   10. Umlauf Sculpture Garden & Museum 17
   11. Barton Springs Municipal Pool 18
   12. The Boardwalk at Lady Bird Lake 20
   13. Lou Neff Point 21
   14. Mount Bonnell 23
   15. Pennybacker Bridge 24

BEAUMONT
   16. Fire Museum of Texas 25
   17. Cattail Marsh Scenic Wetlands & Boardwalk 26
   18. Beaumont Botanical Gardens 28

BROWNSVILLE
   19. Boca Chica Beach 29
   20. Resaca de la Palma State Park 31
   21. Palo Alto Battlefield National Historical Park 32
   22. Palmito Ranch Battlefield 34
   23. Sabal Palm Sanctuary 35

COLLEGE STATION
   24. Texas A&M Bonfire Memorial 37
   25. Brazos Valley Veterans Memorial 39

CORPUS CHRISTI
26. Corpus Christi Downtown Seawall...40
27. South Texas Music Walk of Fame 42
28. Mustang Island State Park 43
29. Watergardens Fountains 45

DALLAS
30. Reunion Tower 46
31. Bishop Arts District..48
32. Dallas Arboretum and Botanical Gardens 49
33. Dealey Plaza National Historic Landmark District 51
34. The Dallas World Aquarium 52
35. Dallas Zoo 54
36. Dallas Cattle Drive Sculptures..55
37. Fountain Place 56
38. White Rock Lake 57
39. Trinity Groves 59
40. Giant Eyeball 61
41. Hall of State..62
42. Thanks-Giving Square 63
43. Nasher Sculpture Center 65
44. Grapevine Vintage Railroad 66

DEL RIO
45. Devils River State Natural Area 68
46. Dolan Falls 69
47. Lake Amistad National Recreation Area...70

EL PASO
48. Chamizal National Memorial 71
49. Magoffin Home State Historic Site 72
50. Old Fort Bliss Replica 73
51. Hueco Tanks State Historic Site 74

FORT DAVIS
52. McDonald Observatory 75
53. Chihuahuan Desert Nature Center..76
54. Davis Mountain State Park...77
55. Fort Davis National Historic Site 79

FORT WORTH
56. Fort Worth Botanic Garden..80
58. Fort Worth Nature Center & Refuge 82
58. Fort Worth Stockyards 83
59. Marion Sansom Park 84
60. The Ball-Eddleman-McFarland House 85
61. Log Cabin Village 86

FREDERICKSBURG
- 62. Enchanted Rock State Natural Area 87
- 63. Wildseed Farms 89
- 64. Pioneer Museum 90
- 65. Fort Martin Scott 92
- 66. Willow City Loop 93

GALVESTON
- 67. 1892 Bishop's Palace 94
- 68. The Seawall 95
- 69. Moody Mansion 96
- 70. Galveston's 61st Street Fishing Pier 97

GEORGETOWN
- 71. Central Texas Olive Ranch 98
- 72. Historic Williamson County Courthouse 99
- 73. Inner Space Cavern 101

GRANBURY
- 74. Granbury City Beach Park 102

HOUSTON
- 75. Buffalo Soldiers National Museum 104
- 76. Space Center Houston 105
- 77. Sam Houston Park 107
- 78. Battleship Texas 108

JOHNSON CITY
- 79. Pedernales Falls State Park 109

KARNAK
- 80. Caddo Lake State Park 110

KEMAH
- 81. Kemah Boardwalk 111

KOUNTZE
- 82. Roy E. Larsen Sandyland Sanctuary 112

LOMETA
- 83. Gorman Falls 113

MARFA
- 84. Marfa Lights Viewing Area 114

MATAGORDA
- 85. Matagorda Bay Nature Park 115

NEW BRAUNFELS
- 86. Gruene Historic District 117

ODESSA
87. Stonehenge Replica 118

PITTSBURG
88. Lake Bob Sandlin State Park 119

PORT ARANSAS
89. Port Aransas Fishermans Wharf 120

PORT LAVACA
90. Halfmoon Reef Lighthouse 121

POTTSBORO
91. Island View Park 123

SAN ANTONIO
92. Mcnay Art Museum 124
93. Camanche Lookout Park 126
94. Pearl Brewery 127
95. Market Square(El Mercado) 129
96. San Antonio River Walk 130
97. San Antonio Mission National Historical Park 132
98. Tower of Americas 133

SONORA
99. Eaton Hill Nature Center & Preserve 134
100. Caverns of Sonora 135

SPICEWOOD
101. Krause Springs 136
102. Pace Bend Park 137

SUGAR LAND
103. Sugar Land Town Square 138

TERLINGUA
104. Far Flung Outdoor Center 139
105. Big Bend National Park 140

VANDERPOOL
106. Lone Star Motorcycle Museum and Hall of Fame 141
107. Lost Maples State Natural Area 142

WACO
108. Magnolia Market at the Silos 143

WIMBERLEY
109. Jacob's Well 144

ZAVALLA
110. Boykin Springs Recreation Area 145

THE PRIMEVELER TEXAS TRIPS PROPOSAL **146**
   1. The Best Way to Discover Texas Week Itinerary 146
   2. Knowing Texas Week Itinerary 148

Download your Packing Checklist here! **151**

INTRODUCTION

Every year people ask themselves, "What should I do to enjoy my day/month/year?" Well, you can either waste your time on social media, or you could spend it exploring new places! The Texas Bucket List Guide Book is a fantastic guide to all the best places you should visit in Lone Star State. This detailed book will help you decide what places you have to visit. With over 150 places, you will be sure to be entertained for days!

The Texas Bucket List Guide Book will remove any excuse from people who want something more out of their lives. You will no longer have to pass up a trip because it's not "worth it," or "too expensive," or "too far away." You're sure to appreciate the various adventures and never get bored.

You'll always be able to experience the latest attraction because of your location. The thing people most often complain about when traveling is that they wish they saw more of what their destination offered. By using this guidebook, you will spend less time planning and more time exploring.

The list includes iconic places and hidden gems that even the locals don't know about. This book will help anyone travel all over Texas in the most effective way possible. Get ready for an adventure you'll never forget!

ABOUT TEXAS

"Texas" is derived from the Caddo Indian word "tayshas" which means "friends" or "allies," which is how the Indians and the first European settlers viewed each other.

On December 29, 1845, Texas became the 28th state. It had been free from Mexico for ten years at this point. During that time, Texas was its own country, which is why people all over the state were very proud of their state. This is the only state in the United States that was once its own nation. The state flag of Texas, which is called the "Lone Star State," is the flag of independence from Mexico. It's a sign of how independent Texans are. Texas has always been a place where people seek adventure and new experiences, from its early days as a frontier town to its current status as one of the largest states in the United States.

Texas has the second-largest population in the United States, with over 29 million residents, or 6.8% of the total population. It is the second-largest state in the United States. Austin is the state capital, but Houston is the most populous city in Texas, with a population of over 2.3 million. Houston, San Antonio, and Dallas are the three cities with populations surpassing one million in Texas. The state is in the south-central part of the United States of America. It is 696,241 km² in size and takes up 7% of the United States. Louisiana, Arkansas, Oklahoma, and New Mexico are all close to Texas.

Texas is more than just a large state with a population that rivals states like California and New York. It's also known for its rich and diverse culture, with a variety of cuisine, art scenes, music and dance styles, and many other things to offer.

CLIMATE AND LANDSCAPE

One of the most beautiful things about Texas is its landscape and climate. As you travel throughout the state, you'll find that it's a land of contrasts: from the desert to the coast, from the rolling plains to the mountains, from forests to cacti and grasslands--you can go anywhere in Texas and find something new and different.

The best time to go to Texas is in the summer when there are lots of festivals, music events, and things to do outside. Many events are held at state parks, including rodeos and car shows. As the temperature climbs in the summer, many people spend their spare time outdoors and enjoy barbecues or picnics. In springtime, there are festivals that celebrate all kinds of nature--from wildlife to plant life. Even fall is a great season to visit Texas: It's still warm enough to photograph things like pumpkins and leaves, but it also has beautiful colors as the season changes into winter.

The Texas climate can be classified as humid subtropical. The climate in the state is hot and humid. The heat from the sun makes it difficult to keep cool. In the summer, temperatures often hit into the 100s Fahrenheit at night, and it's not hard to find a stream or lake where you can cool off. To escape the heat, you might look for museums, go hiking, try rock climbing, or swim in a lake.

Texas has many different ecosystems, which means that you can see different kinds of birds, animals, plants, and even trees all over the state. You can find everything from the Everglades in the south to the prairies of the north. In addition to large animals like bears and elk, Texas is home to a variety of birds and even some bats. Many types of plants and trees can be found in Texas, including oaks, pines, cacti, cypresses, and palms.

It has everything from the desert to the mountainous regions and the coast. In fact, some people come to Texas looking for beach communities. The beaches in Texas are usually short and narrow because most of the population is in landlocked areas, but there are still miles of coastline that have been made popular by surfers and individuals who want to spend a day at the beach. Some towns in Texas have great nightlife, while others are quiet and perfect for relaxing. One town might be known as a music haven, while another is known for its art community. You will always find something new no matter what city or town you visit in Texas. It's one of the most diverse states in America, both culturally and geographically speaking.

THE MAP OF TEXAS

Source: GISGeography.com

HOW TO USE THIS GUIDE

This guide is designed to be a comprehensive resource for anyone looking to make the most of their time in Texas. Whether you're planning a trip or want to know what's around town, this guide has got you covered. It includes information on why you should visit the place, where exactly the location of the place is, the best time to visit if there is a requirement that is needed to enter the place, the closest city or town, and a bit of fact about that place.

As this guide is sorted based on what region of the state each place is in, you'll find that some of the places listed are near more than one region. As you read through this guide and discover new places, I recommend that you take notes and make a list of your favorite places to visit in Texas, as at the end of the guide is a journal page for you to do so. You'll have your own bucket list and can check off sites to visit as you go. It's a fantastic way to learn more about the state and keep in mind exciting places to visit.

GPS coordinates have been included where possible so that you can find these places without any issues. Most of the cities and towns in Texas are fairly fast to navigate, but some of these locations may present some challenges--especially those in the more isolated areas.

Luckily, technology has advanced to the point where GPS coordinates are now a norm for most mobile devices, even those found on phones. You can use Google Maps or download an app like GPS Navigator if you have an Android device. You can easily get the coordinates for any place in the world via most of these apps. You can use any app that Apple makes if you have an iPhone. They have their own GPS system within the phone itself. You'll have to enter your destination as a place name or address and add the term "GPS" after it. The app will give you the coordinates and then direct you to the place that you're looking for.

1. CADILLAC RANCH

Why You Should Visit:
Cadillac Ranch is a must-see attraction in Texas. It's best known as a "graffiti gallery," where visitors can see some of the best work done by some of today's most famous artists. The site has long been a popular stop for out-of-town motorists and even celebrities. It is a series of art installations made from old Cadillacs that have been painted and placed in the landscape. The sculptures are meant to be viewed from above or below, but they also serve as a reminder of how our society views luxury cars-- as symbols of success and status rather than functional transportation devices.

Location:
13651 I-40 Frontage Rd, Amarillo, TX 79124, United States

Best Time To Visit:
Year-round, but best during fall/spring because there is less chance of it being too hot or too cold.

Pass/Permit/Fees:
Free

How to Get There:
From most of Texas's big cities, you can get to US-287 North by taking 1-45 or 1-35 West. The route starts in Wichita Falls and ends in Amarillo. Take Exit 63 off of 1-40 West. Find the statue of the Second Amendment Cowboy by the gift shop.

GPS Coordinates:
35.1872° N, 101.9870° W

Closest City or Town:
The closest city is Amarillo, which is about 45 minutes away. The other cities of Texas that nearby include Lubbock, Dalhart, and Borger. Lubbock is about three hours away, while Dallhart and Borger are about two hours away. The closest metropolitan area to Cadillac Ranch is the Dallas/Fort Worth area.

Did You Know:

This roadside attraction began as a prank by artist Robert "Bob" Marley, who spray-painted his car with the word Cadillac and drove it onto the road in 1970. Since then, it has grown into an internationally recognized symbol of rebellion against consumerism and materialism.

2. AMARILLO BOTANICAL GARDEN

Why You Should Visit:

Amarillo Botanical Garden is a must-visit for any traveler in Texas. The Garden is stunning, with its lush green lawns and winding paths. It is also home to many beautiful flowers and plants that are not commonly found in other parts of the state. Its grounds have many different paths, so you can choose your own adventure if you want to. There are also many different exhibits that change throughout the year, so there's always something new to see!

Location:

1400 Streit Dr, Amarillo, TX 79106, United States

Best Time To Visit:

Year-round. Summers are best as it's not too hot or too cold to go inside the botanical gardens. It can get hot in the morning and evening in the summer months, so wear light clothing and bring a hat if you're planning on going there during those times. The grounds of this Garden are huge; they have plenty of space to walk around and enjoy all the flowers in bloom.

Pass/Permit/Fees:

Adults are $5, Seniors (60 and over) $4, 6 - 12 $2, and Children 5 and under are free.

GPS Coordinates:

35.1977° N, 101.9153° W

How to Get There:

On I-40 West, take Exit 223 for Streit Drive. Turn left onto Streit Drive and followed it to the Gardens' parking lot.

Closest City or Town:

Amarillo is the closest city to the gardens, but there are a few large towns in Texas that are nearby. The closest big city to the gardens is El Paso, which is about three and a half hours away.

Did You Know:

The garden's more than 200 species make up Texas's largest collection of plants. You'll find the most common garden plants like roses, azaleas, and hydrangeas here as well as rare species like the Lady Banksia tree (which is only found in Australia). There are also wide varieties of cacti from all over the world.

3. PALO DURO CANYON STATE PARK

If you want to see the stunning natural areas of Texas and learn about its history, visit Palo Duro Canyon State Park. The park encompasses over 700,000 acres of wilderness and is home to several species of endangered plants and animals. It also contains some of the oldest geologic formations in North America, including the famous "pothole" caves that were formed by hot springs millions of years ago. The park's most famous feature is its canyon walls, which rise up from an elevation at the base of Texas Hill Country at around 2,000 feet above sea level to over 4,300 feet at their highest point.

Location:

11450 State Hwy Park Rd 5, Canyon, TX 79015, United States

GPS Coordinates:

34.9373° N, 101.6589° W

How to Get There:

About 12 miles east of Canyon, on State Highway 217, is Palo Duro Canyon State Park. Take I-27 south from Amarillo to State Highway 217, then go east for 8 miles.

Pass/Permit/Fees:

$8 for 13 and older

Closest City or Town:

It's only 25 miles from downtown Amarillo and 14 miles from Canyon's Mainstreet.

Did You Know:

The cliffs in this place are so high that they block out much sunlight during summer months (when they're still covered with snow), making it difficult for plants and animals living inside them to survive without access to sunlight or other sources of energy such as heat from geothermal activity below ground level where water seeps through cracks in rocks or outer layers of earth crust itself! Many plants and animals go dormant during the winter months and rely on geothermal energy below ground level to keep them warm enough to survive through the cold winter months.

4. TEXAS AIR & SPACE MUSEUM

If you love planes, rockets, and astronauts, then the Texas Air & Space Museum is a must-visit. The museum houses an extensive collection of aircraft, spacecraft, and space artifacts worldwide. There are also many interactive exhibits that educate visitors about the history of aviation and space exploration.

Location:

10001 American Dr, Amarillo, TX 79111, United States

GPS Coordinates:

35.2134° N, 101.7140° W

How to Get There:

Follow I-40 east for about 7 miles to exit 76. Turn left onto Airport Blvd and drive north/northeast for about 1.5 miles when you get off. Then, turn left and follow Tiltrotor Dr. to 10001 American Dr.

Pass/Permit/Fees:

Admission is free admission, but donations are accepted.

Closest City or Town:

Amarillo is the closest city to the museum, but there are many other towns in Texas that are nearby. The closest big cities to the museum are Dallas, which is about 3 hours away, and Austin, which is about 5 hours away.

Did You Know:

The museum has many exhibits, but the Space Shuttle Pavilion is the most popular. It houses a real NASA space shuttle that was used to perform numerous missions in Earth's orbit. There's also an exhibit of a simulator that teaches visitors how astronauts train for their space missions. Visitors can also get up close and personal with an original Apollo command module and many other exotic aircraft.

5. SIX FLAGS OVER TEXAS

Why You Should Visit:

If you're looking for a place to go that's fun, exciting, and full of thrills, Six Flags Over Texas is the place for you! It has several roller coasters and other rides for all ages to enjoy. They also have an arcade room where kids can play games like Ms. Pacman and Galaga while adults can enjoy some classic video games such as Donkey Kong or Donkey Kong Jr.

The best part about Six Flags Over Texas is the food! There are many different options, including burgers, hot dogs, pizza slices, or even ice cream cones! If you don't want to wait in line at one of their restaurants, then there are plenty of other places nearby where you can grab some food on-site before or after your ride or game.

Location:

2201 E Road to Six Flags St, Arlington, TX 76011, United States

Best Time To Visit:

Spring, summer, and fall are best because the park is not too hot or too cold-there's even a water park to help you beat the heat! You can also go during winter as long as you bring some warm clothes; they get pretty chilly at night!

Pass/Permit/Fees:

Prices on One-Day tickets range from $25 to $90

How to Get There:

If you are coming from Huntsville or Houston, take I-45 north until you reach I-20. Take I-20 west toward Dallas-Fort Worth until you reach the DFW Airport exit (State Highway 360 North). Take 360 north for about six miles, and then take the exit for I-30 (Six Flags) on the right. Follow the signs to get there.

GPS Coordinates:

32.7550° N, 97.0703° W

Closest City or Town:

Arlington is the closest big city to Six Flags Over Texas, but it is still about an hour's drive. Other Texas cities nearby include Fort Worth and Dallas. Both are about 45 minutes away from the park each way. If you're coming from Huntsville, TX, the closest major town is Longview, which is about a 1-hour drive away.

Did You Know:

Six Flags Over Texas actually has two entrances: Main Entrance and Front Gate.

The main entrance is on the west side of the park. This is where you'll find the ticket booths, dining area, and gift shops. Because of this, this entrance is always very crowded. If you want to avoid dealing with crowds, then use the front gate entrance-it's about a mile away from the main entrance, and it's a much more peaceful experience.

6. ARLINGTON MUSEUM OF ART

It is one of the finest museums in Texas, and it houses an incredible collection of art from around the globe. The museum has works by masters like Rembrandt van Rijn and Vincent van Gogh, but it also has some modern favorites like Pablo Picasso, who painted his most famous work here in Arlington.

The museum also has a great Greek and Roman art collection, which is just as impressive as anything else in its collection. You can see sculptures from ancient Greece, like sculptures by Praxiteles or Lysippos, at this museum--they're both incredibly beautiful pieces that will take your breath away when you see them up close. If you're looking for something different from what's offered at other museums around town, check out this one!

Location:
201 W Main St, Arlington, TX 76010, United States

Best Time To Visit:
To see all of the museum's exhibits, visit during weekdays. You'll also be able to see more pieces from the museum's collection if you go this time as well.

Pass/Permit/Fees:
Seniors (age 55+): $15.00; Adults (ages 19-54): $20.00; Youth (ages 13-18): $15.00; Children (ages 2-12): $5.00; Infants (ages 0-1): free.

How to Get There:
From I-20, go north on State Highway 360 and turn right onto S. Collins Street. Then turn right onto W Main Street to the museum, which is located immediately on your left.

GPS Coordinates:
32.733° N, 97.109° W

Closest City or Town:
A few small towns in Texas are nearby, but Arlington is the closest city to the museum- about 1 minute away from it! The next largest town is Grand Prairie, TX, and it's about a 10-minute drive from there to the museum.

Did You Know:
In addition to its impressive collection of artworks, the Arlington Museum of Art has several special exhibitions throughout the year that feature works by local artists or highlight specific themes like nature or mythology.

7. MCKINNEY FALLS STATE PARK

Why You Should Visit:

McKinney Falls State Park is not only a beautiful place to visit, but it is also one of the best places to witness the natural beauty of Texas. The park features three waterfalls that can be seen from the parking lot. The Trinity River and McKinney Creek feed the falls. The tallest waterfall, called "Old Mill," towers over 200 feet high. The second-tallest waterfall is called "Saddlebag Falls." It's only about half as tall as Old Mill, but it has a much more impressive appearance because it drops straight down from a cliff face instead of falling over an edge as Old Mill does.

Location:

5808 McKinney Falls Pkwy, Austin, TX 78744, United States

Best Time To Visit:

Between April and October, when there are fewer visitors than at other times of the year, is the best time to visit McKinney Falls State Park.

Pass/Permit/Fees:

For ages 13 and above: $6.25

How to Get There:

The park is on U.S. Highway 183, 13 miles southeast of the state capital in Austin. From U.S. 183 South, take McKinney Falls Parkway straight to the park entrance.

GPS Coordinates:

30.1836° N, 97.7222° W

Closest City or Town:

While McKinney Falls State Park is near Austin, TX, it's about a 40-minute drive from the state capital. Another nearby town like, Georgetown, TX, is only 14 minutes away.

Did You Know:

The area around McKinney Falls State Park is home to many species of animals, including deer, rabbits, squirrels, raccoons, and snakes. You can also see different kinds of birds, including hawks or bald eagles, flying overhead!

8. BULLOCK TEXAS STATE HISTORY MUSEUM

Why You Should Visit:

If you're looking for a place to get away and learn about Texas history, the Bullock Texas State History Museum is the place for you.

The museum, which opened in 2014, is housed in an old cotton warehouse and has been named one of the best museums in America by The Smithsonian Institution. The building was built in 1892 and served as a storage facility until it was converted into a museum.

The museum's collection includes artifacts from all over Texas, including items from Native Americans and Spanish explorers who traveled through the state during its early history. It also holds exhibits on things like local historical figures like Lyndon Baines Johnson and George W Bush, who both served as president at different times during their lives.

Location:

1800 Congress Ave., Austin, TX 78701, United States

Best Time To Visit:

Tuesday is the best day to visit the museum since they host a special lecture that showcases how Texas has developed into what it is today. Check the schedule of events on the museum's website and make a plan to visit during one of those days.

Pass/Permit/Fees:

For adults: $13; For students, military, or senior (age 65+): $11; For ages 4-17: $9

How to Get There:

If you're driving from far away, I-35 is a safer bet. If you're coming from the north (Fort Worth area), take exit number one for Congress and turn right onto Congress. Then turn left onto 18th Street and then turn right onto the museum's address.

GPS Coordinates:

30.2803° N, 97.7391° W

Closest City or Town:

The next closest city is San Marcos, TX, which is about 16 miles from the museum.

Did You Know:

The museum has over 400,000 artifacts on display that the Bullock family collected over the years. It also has a small planetarium and an exhibit on the history of Texas that is worth checking out as well.

9. TEXAS CAPITOL

Why You Should Visit:
One of the most iconic landmarks in Texas, the Capitol Building is a must for any bucket list. The building was completed in 1871 and has been home to many important events in Texas history, including the signing of the Texas Declaration of Independence, which was signed here by Sam Houston on February 24th, 1836. It also served as a prison during the American Civil War when it was used as a military hospital.

Location:
1100 Congress Ave., Austin, TX 78701, United States

Best Time To Visit:
The best time to visit the Texas Capitol Building is during the spring and fall when it's not so hot in Austin. It's also nice in the winter since it has a beautiful Christmas-themed display outside of the building.

Pass/Permit/Fees:
Capitol Tours are free

How to Get There:
If you're coming from Austin, take I-35 to exit number 236. After your exit, turn left onto 11th Street and then turn right onto Congress Avenue. Once you reach the intersection with 11th Street, turn left onto Congress Avenue, then continue until you reach the intersection with Guadalupe Street. Turn right at this intersection to enter the Capitol grounds on your right-hand side.

GPS Coordinates:
30.2747° N, 97.7404° W

Closest City or Town:
The closest city, Round Rock, is located 10 miles to the east.

Did You Know:
There are over 1,000 rooms inside the Texas State Capitol Building, which is one of its most intriguing features. Some of them have never even been opened since they were built!

10. UMLAUF SCULPTURE GARDEN & MUSEUM

Why You Should Visit:

If you're looking for a unique experience that's sure to make your jaw drop, look no further than the Umlauf Sculpture Garden & Museum. This museum is home to over 800 pieces of art by renowned sculptor Charles Umlauf and his wife, Lila Umlauf. If you love art but only have time for a part day of museums, then this would be a great place to visit on your Texas Bucket List!

Location:

605 Azie Morton Rd, Austin, TX 78704, United States

Best Time To Visit:

The sculpture garden is open year-round except on Christmas Day. The best time to visit the gardens is March through October. It's a lovely spot to visit during the holidays because the garden is illuminated in the winter to produce a stunning spectacle.

Pass/Permit/Fees:

Children that are ages 0-12 years old, veterans, active military: free; for ages 13-17 years: $1; for 60+: $5; for students: $3.00; for adults: $7.00.

How to Get There:

GPS Coordinates:

30.2633° N, 97.7662° W

Closest City or Town:

The next largest nearby town is Georgetown, TX, which is about an hour away from downtown Austin.

Did You Know:

During their lifetime, Charles Umlauf and Lila Umlauf donated over 60 pieces of art to the city of Austin. From sculptures to paintings and even jewelry, every piece in the museum's collection has been donated by the couple.

11. BARTON SPRINGS MUNICIPAL POOL

Why You Should Visit:

The pool is located in the heart of Austin, Texas, and it's a must-visit for any visitor looking to experience the city's best attractions. The pool is home to one of the most beautiful natural springs in all of Texas. The water flows from deep underground through an underground tunnel into the Barton Springs Pool, where it flows into a large outdoor pool with a fountain at its center.

Location:

2201 William Barton Dr, Austin, TX 78746, United States

Best Time To Visit:

The pool is open from March through October on weekdays and weekends, but the best time to visit is during the spring and fall. Summer can get pretty hot in Austin, so if you prefer to stay cool, it is recommended to visit in March or October when it's cooler!

Pass/Permit/Fees:

After 8 a.m. on Tuesdays, Fridays, Saturdays, and Sundays, Barton Springs requires a valid entry pass. For residents, children that are ages 1-11 years old: 2=$2; for ages 12-17 years: $3; for ages 18-62 years: $5; for ages 62 years and older; for veterans(honorably discharged) and children under 1 year: free.

For non-residents, children that are ages 1-11 years old: 2=$4; for ages 12-17 years: $5; for ages 18-62 years: $9; for ages 62 years and older; for veterans(honorably discharged) and children under 1 year: free.

How to Get There:

The Barton Springs Pool is located just north of the Capitol Building, and it's about a 10-minute walk from the center of downtown Austin. If you're coming from the North, take I-35 to exit number 236 for Guadalupe Street East. From there, turn right onto Guadalupe and then left up William Barton Drive when you see the sign for Barton Springs Pool on your left side.

GPS Coordinates:

30.2641° N, 97.7713° W

Closest City or Town:

The next largest nearby city is Leander, TX, which is about a 20-minute drive from downtown Austin.

Did You Know:
It's one of the oldest municipal pools in the country, and it has a history of being used by locals as a warm-up spot before going to the Austin City Limits Music Festival.

12. THE BOARDWALK AT LADY BIRD LAKE

Why You Should Visit:
The Boardwalk at Lady Bird Lake is a great place to visit because it's a popular destination for people of all ages. Whether you're a family looking for an afternoon out or a couple looking to take a romantic stroll, this park is the perfect spot! The Boardwalk features restaurants, shops, museums, and outdoor art galleries. You can walk around the lake's edge and look at the beautiful skyline of the city. There are also fun activities such as paddle boating and pedal boating.

Location:
1820 S Lakeshore Blvd, Austin, TX 78741

Best Time to Visit:
Anytime is a good time to visit Boardwalk park because it has outdoor weather amenities. It's also open at night during the summer thanks to its live music events happening on the pier. If you plan to visit when it's dark out, be extra careful! While the park is pretty safe during the day, it isn't too safe for young children at night. If you have kids who are afraid of the dark, try going during the day! This will make everyone feel more comfortable and safe.

Pass/Permit/Fees:
The Boardwalk is free of charge, although you'll have to pay for fun activities such as paddle and pedal boating.

How to Get There:
To get to the Boardwalk, you can start at Lake Austin Boulevard. It's right off Interstate 35, so it's easy to find. If you're coming from downtown Austin, then you can head north on I-35 until you reach the South First Street exit. Take a left onto South First Street and go until you reach Lake Austin Boulevard. Take a right onto Lake Austin Blvd and drive for about 4 miles until you see the park on your left!

GPS Coordinates:
30° 15' 1.80" N, -97° 42' 29.39" W

Closest City or Town:
The next closest city over is Georgetown, TX, about three miles to the northwest of the park.

Did You Know:
Lady Bird Lake is a man-made lake that was created in 1960. The lake's surface area is 416 acres (168 ha), with a depth of 9.4 feet (2.87 m). The Colorado River flows into the lake. It starts at the Highland Dam and Spillway, which is right next to the city of Austin

13. LOU NEFF POINT

Why You Should Visit:

The Lou Neff Point is a place that you'll want to visit if you're in Austin. It's a beautiful spot where you can see the city skyline and enjoy the views of Lake Travis. The point has been named after Lou Neff, a pioneer in Austin's development.

The point is on Lake Travis, making it a great spot for fishing and boating. It's also popular for hiking and picnicking because of its scenic views.

Location:

Ann and Roy Butler Hike and Bike Trail, Austin, TX 78746, United States

Best Time To Visit:

You should visit this park anytime during the year, but the best time to do so is when there is no rain, like in the months of April and May. April is especially great because the water levels are low, which makes it easy for you to get to the point and visit.

Pass/Permit/Fees:

There's no charge to get into the park, so there's no need to fuss about paying a fee. You can rent a boat or use the fishing hole for free, but if you want to picnic or bring your own boat, then you'll have to pay for it.

How to Get There:

Take I-35 south from downtown Austin to exit 50, which is the Highland Mall exit. Take a left on FM-350. Follow that road into Lake Travis (that's Highway 611). After that, there's a trailhead where you can park your car and get started on your hike or bike ride. This is an expansive lake, and you'll want to take some time to get around it before heading back into town. The trailhead is located at 7201 Highway 611 between Lake Austin Dam Loop and Rainbow Bend Hospital (located near Round Rock).

GPS Coordinates:

30.2672° N, 97.7617° W

Closest City or Town:

The city of Round Rock, TX, is about 30 minutes away from the park, and it's located on Highway 6.

Did You Know:

Many people visit Lou Neff Point to see the area's famous willow and cottonwood trees. These trees are over 300 years old, so they are considered to be some of the oldest living things in the world.

14. MOUNT BONNELL

Why You Should Visit:

If you're looking for mountain views without having to go too far out of town, visit Mount Bonnell. This Austin overlook is located alongside the Lake Austin portion of the Colorado River and offers a breathtaking view of the city below. You can also see the Colorado River and enjoy some excellent hiking trails nearby.

Location:

3800 Mt. Bonnell Drive, Austin, TX, 78731

Best Time to Visit:

Mount Bonnell is constantly lovely, making spring and summer ideal times to visit. All of the foliage is changing and filled with vibrant colors, so this is a great time to enjoy the scenery! You can also hike during this time too; the trails are less crowded, and you can enjoy the scenery from a closer vantage point.

Pass/Permit/Fees:

There is no fee to visit Mount Bonnell, although there is a parking fee of $7.

How to Get There:

To get to Mount Bonnel, you'll want to head south on Loop 360 toward Highway 71. Take Highway 71 until you reach the intersection with Mount Bonnell Road. Turn right and follow the road until it ends at a parking lot with an entrance and a wrought iron gate. If you ever get lost, your best bet is to ask someone for directions.

GPS Coordinates:

30.3210°N, 97.7736°W

Closest City or Town:

The next town over is Bee Cave, TX, and it's about a 10-minute drive from Mount Bonnell.

Did You Know:

Mount Bonnell is named after a military man named George Bonnell. He was the first commissioner of the Texas Rangers and died in 1845 while leading a military expedition to   de Bexar, which is now known as San Antonio, TX. The Comanche Indians decapitated him, so naturally, this was a huge loss for the Texas Army.

15. PENNYBACKER BRIDGE

Why You Should Visit:

The 360 Bridge in Austin has beautiful views of downtown Austin, and the sunset is a great time to see it. If you want a romantic place to watch the sunset with someone special, this is it! It's also a popular place for marriage proposals, so if you want to pop the question, this is the best place to do it!

Location:

5300 N Capital of Texas Hwy, Austin, TX 78730

Best Time to Visit:

The best time to visit Pennybacker Bridge is during the day or at sunset. The months of March and April are great times to visit because it's springtime, and the weather is gorgeous!

Pass/Permit/Fees:

There is no charge for parking in the park, but the bridge does cost $3 to enter.

There's a restroom in the park office, so remember to use it. While you're there, you can also take a look inside the office and see some of the awesome things they have on display!

How to Get There:

The bridge is located near Lake Austin Boulevard and sits right on top of it. Take Loop 360 North until you reach the Capital of Texas Highway (Highway 71). Take a left onto Cap of Texas Highway. Follow this road until you reach the bridge. It's easy to find since it's one of the most photographed places in Austin.

GPS Coordinates:

30° 20' 49.4052" N, 97° 48' 0.6264" W

Closest City or Town:

The next closest city over is Dripping Springs, TX, which is located all the way to the southeast of Austin.

Did You Know:

The Pennybacker Bridge was built in 1973 to replace a nearby bridge that was destroyed by a fire. Before the bridge was built, you couldn't see the downtown area from there. There used to be many more businesses located around the bridge; now, there's only one restaurant left. Another thing you might need to learn is that this bridge is named after George Pennybacker, who donated $800,000 for its construction!

16. FIRE MUSEUM OF TEXAS

Why You Should Visit:
If you have an interest in the fire service and firefighting in Texas, the Fire Museum of Texas is the place for you. This museum features many different items from the state's past and present fire departments. You'll even be able to tour some of their fire trucks and take a look at a few fire engines as well!

Location:
400 Walnut St Beaumont, TX, Beaumont, TX 77701-2344

Best Time to Visit:
The Fire Museum of Texas is open on weekdays from 8 am to 4:30 pm. It is open year-round, but if you're looking for a unique experience, visit between the months of October and April, when the museum is decorated for Halloween. You can also catch them during Fire Prevention Week or Texas Firefighters Museum Month!

Pass/Permit/Fees:
Free admission is granted to visitors with valid driver's licenses or state IDs. All visitors must be at least 7 years of age to enter the museum. You'll need to purchase an annual pass if you want to visit more than one time! The pass costs $15 and can be purchased online or at the museum.

How to Get There:
The museum is located in Beaumont, just a short ride from I-10. Take Interstate 10 East until you reach Interstate 10 West. Exit at Walnut Street and follow Walnut St. all the way until you reach Main St., where you'll make a right turn onto Walnut Street. Make the first left onto Chestnut St, and then make another left onto Sallisaw Ave. After the road curves around, make a left onto Palm St. and then make another left onto Walnut St. The museum is located on the right. You can't miss it!

GPS Coordinates:
30° 5' 9.4776" N, 94° 5' 54.7512" W

Closest City or Town:
The Fire Museum of Texas is in Beaumont, TX. Orange, TX, is 7 miles away, and Port Arthur, TX, is 11 miles away. If you're coming from Louisiana, the museum is only 15 minutes away from Vidor and just 25 minutes away from Jefferson Parish, LA.

Did You Know:
You can see the world's largest working fire hydrate that Disney donated in 1999. It's still operational and running on a large diesel engine that powers the fire hydrant. There is also a fully functional city fire station and an interesting collection of different firefighting tools!

17. CATTAIL MARSH SCENIC WETLANDS & BOARDWALK

Why You Should Visit:

If you're looking for a place to spend some time in the great outdoors, look no further than Cattail Marsh Scenic Wetlands & Boardwalk. This park is located in Texas, and it's known for its beautiful scenery and wildlife. The boardwalk winds through the marshland, allowing you to see all kinds of animals up close. You can also go hiking or biking on one of their trails, which are perfect for people of all levels.

Location:

6088 Babe Zaharias Drive, Beaumont, Texas

Best Time to Visit:

If you visit in the fall, spring, or summer, it's best to visit during daylight hours because it's stifling hot! If you're looking to avoid the heat, you should definitely check out Cattail Marsh in the wintertime. It can get cold overnight and snow in the winter months! The marsh is also beautiful at night and lit up by thousands of lanterns.

Pass/Permit/Fees:

There are no fees that are required for admission. However, if you want to explore some of their trails and check out their facilities and exhibits, you'll need to purchase a pass for $10.

How to Get There:

Cattail Marsh Scenic Wetlands & Boardwalk is only a short drive away from Beaumont and Orange, TX. Take Interstate 10 East until you reach Interstate 10 West. Exit at Campbell Drive (Exit 7) and follow the road until you reach Fairfield Avenue. Turn right and make another right onto Cattail Road. You'll pass the Johnson Space Center on your left and see Two Rivers Lake on your right. Turn right onto Eastman Road and follow the road until you reach Babe Zaharias Drive. Make a right turn and then make another right turn onto Babe Zaharias Drive to park at the boardwalk.

GPS Coordinates:

30° 0' 28" N, 94° 8' 34" W

Closest City or Town:

Cattail Marsh Scenic Wetlands & Boardwalk is located in Beaumont, which is about 20 miles away from Orange, TX, and 25 miles away from Port Arthur, TX.

Did You Know:

The boardwalk that runs through the marshland was built with the help of inmates from the nearby Beaumont prison. They are also responsible for building a wheelchair-accessible trail, which allows visitors to hike or bike through a part of the marshland on a paved road. They received a grant for $40,000 from TX Parks & Wildlife in order to make this happen!

18. BEAUMONT BOTANICAL GARDENS

Why You Should Visit:

Beaumont Botanical Gardens is the perfect place to explore the beautiful world of plants. This garden has over 1,000 different species of trees, shrubs, and flowers throughout its grounds--and they're all located in one place!

The gardens are filled with walking paths and trails that lead through various parts of the garden. You can also get up close to some of your favorite trees, like oaks, sycamores, and cedars. If you want to do something more hands-on, there's even an arboretum where you can learn how to identify trees and take care of plants.

Location:

6088 Babe Zaharias Drive, Tyrrell Park, Beaumont, Texas

Best Time to Visit:

If you're visiting between October and March, you'll have to check the weather because the gardens are closed for winter! If you're looking for something beautiful all year round, come visit in the spring. Some of their flowers may still be in full bloom during this time of year!

Pass/Permit/Fees:

There are no fees required for admission, but if you'd like to explore some of the attractions and facilities, you'll need to purchase a pass. The Adult Day Pass is $8, while the Adult Month Pass is $38. The Day pass gives you access to the interactive arboretum, the butterfly pavilion, and a picnic area. It also allows you to walk around on one of their trails or explore their rose garden.

How to Get There:

You can find it by taking the exit off of Interstate 10 East onto Interstate 10 West. Exit at Walnut Street and follow Walnut St. all the way until you reach Main St., where you'll make a right turn onto Walnut Street. Make the first left onto Chestnut St, and then make another left onto Sallisaw Ave. After the road curves around, make a left onto Palm St. and then make another left onto Walnut St. The gardens are located on the far west end of this street!

GPS Coordinates:

30.0233°N, 94.1465°W

Closest City or Town:

The next-closest city over is Port Arthur, which is located 45 miles to the northeast.

Did You Know:

The gardens were originally created in the early 1900s by an amateur botanist named William J. Durst. He planted over 4,000 different species of plants and trees, including some that have been extinct for more than 100 years.

19. BOCA CHICA BEACH

Source: William L. Farr

Why You Should Visit:

Boca Chica Beach is the perfect spot to spend a sunny afternoon. The beach is in Texas, and it's known for its beautiful white sand and clear water. There's tons of space to play on the beach, so you'll definitely be able to enjoy this area without any interruption. If you're looking for something more active, there are also opportunities to explore the waters!

Location:

Boca Chica Blvd, Brownsville, TX 78521, USA

Best Time to Visit:

Since the beach isn't located in a city, it's best to visit during daylight hours! If you're looking to go in the wintertime, check the weather and make sure it's a sunny day.

Pass/Permit/Fees:

There are no fees required for admission, but if you'd like to use any of their facilities (like a pool) or explore any of their trails, you'll need a pass! A day pass is $4 for people aged 13 and above, but children aged 12 and younger will get in for free.

How to Get There:

You can find Boca Chica Beach by taking US-83 South and going over the Gulf Intracoastal Waterway. You'll see an exit that says Boca Chica Beaches and Park, so you'll want to take a right at this exit! When you arrive, you'll see a long road that leads to the beach parking lot. There are also multiple places nearby where you can park your car.

GPS Coordinates:

N 25°59.571', W 97°08.915'

Closest City or Town:

The closest city over is Brownsville, TX, which is located just seven miles away. The next-closest city is South Padre Island, which is about 33 miles to the west.

Did You Know:

Boca Chica Beach is home to some of the cleanest and clearest waters due to its protected shoreline. Because the area isn't located near a major city, it's not as polluted as some of the other beaches. The water here is also great for seeing beautiful wildlife like sea turtles, fish, and rays!

20. RESACA DE LA PALMA STATE PARK

Why You Should Visit:

Resaca de la Palma State Park is among the best-kept secrets in the state. It's a small, beautiful park that features scenic views, endangered animals, and plenty of outdoor activities! You can enjoy the tranquility of this area by taking a hike along the park's many trails or by spending time at their campground.

You can do so if you'd like to explore the park on horseback! Guided tours also take you through the area and tell you about its history - it's worth checking out! You can also take advantage of their seasonal lake tours, where you can swim or kayak while learning about the history of the area!

Location:

1000 New Carmen Ave, Brownsville, TX 78521, USA

Best Time to Visit:

This park is open all year round, but it tends to get extremely busy from mid-April to mid-October. If you're planning a visit during these time frames, go in the afternoon or stay away from the weekends.

Pass/Permit/Fees:

When visiting Resaca de la Palma State Park, you'll be required to purchase a pass in order to enter. A one-time pass costs $4 for adults and is free for children under 12 years old.

How to Get There:

From I-35, take the New Carmen exit. Follow the signs for Brownsville and go straight ahead (1 mile). Drive several miles until you reach Resaca de la Palma State Park.

GPS Coordinates:

25° 59' 48.48" N, 97° 34' 17.8536" W.

Did You Know:

Resaca de la Palma was named after a Spanish term meaning "little ravine." Although the park may contain plenty of ravines, this one wasn't named after them! It's named in honor of Salvador Zuno Ruiz, a Spanish colonial governor who operated on this land during this time. The area still holds his name today!

21. PALO ALTO BATTLEFIELD NATIONAL HISTORICAL PARK

Source: Schmorleitz

Why You Should Visit:

This park is a great place to visit for history buffs. This national historic park is the site of the Battle of Palo Alto, which was fought during the Mexican-American War. If you're interested in this battle, you should definitely check out their visitor center! It's full of information on the history of the location and tells visitors about other battles that took place there, such as the Battle of Resaca de la Palma.

The visitor center also provides an overview of the land that this park sits on, including information about the rivers and how they were used for transportation, agriculture, or power generation. The site is also full of exhibits that talk about various aspects of Mexican-American history.

Location:

7200 Paredes Line Rd, Brownsville, TX 78526, USA

Best Time to Visit:

Although the park is open year-round, if you're visiting during the summer or fall months, be prepared for extreme heat. It can get up to 110 degrees in this area during these times! If you want to visit while the weather is decent, visit between October and March. The temperature in this area tends to cool down from April through July, so you won't have to worry about a blazing summer day.

Pass/Permit/Fees:

There is no fee to enter Palo Alto Battlefield or attend park programs and events.

How to Get There:

You can find Palo Alto Battlefield by taking Interstate Highway 83 South and following the signs for Paredes Line Rd. There are numerous parking lots nearby.

GPS Coordinates:

26.0168° N, 97.4790° W

Nearest City or Town:

The next closest town is South Padre Island, located about 38 miles to the east.

Did You Know:

On January 8, 1846, the Battle of Palo Alto commenced. A few days after the battle, a Mexican general named José de Urrea realized that his main force had been defeated and decided to retreat back to Mexico City. He was pursued by the American army and was eventually captured in this area!

22. PALMITO RANCH BATTLEFIELD

Why You Should Visit:

Palmito Ranch Battlefield is one of the best-preserved battlefields in the nation! This area has been preserved thanks to its well-built walls, which were constructed by the Alamo defenders in 1836. These walls are made of limestone quarried from nearby trees. Even so, their imposing sizes make them difficult to see from ground level! No wonder this is one of the most popular places for visitors to visit!

The park also has other buildings that have been preserved and used throughout Texas history: an old mission house, a blacksmith shop, and various outhouses. You can also see the "buffalo wallow," which was used as a bathhouse for buffalos during the Civil War.

Location:

43296 Palmito Hill Rd, Brownsville, TX 78521, USA

Best Time to Visit:

The park is accessible throughout the year, but winter is the greatest time to visit! Snowpack can make it difficult to access the site during this time, but you will still be able to see most of its exterior walls. The spring and fall are also good times to visit, especially between mid-April and mid-October.

Pass/Permit/Fees:

There is no fee to visit Palmito Ranch Battlefield or attend park programs and events.

How to Get There:

Just follow Highway 83 South to Highway 281 and follow the signs for Palmito Hill Rd. Once you reach Palmito Hill Rd, you will see signs for the park, but instead, continue straight. The road loop is about 1 mile long, and then the park will be on your left.

GPS Coordinates:

25° 56' 30.2928" N, 97° 17' 0.9132" W

Nearest City or Town:

The closest city is Pharr, which is about 5 miles away. The closest town is San Juan, which is about 15 miles to the north.

Did You Know:

The Battle of Palmito Ranch took place on January 17, 1836. The Alamo defenders used Palmito Ranch's defensive walls to slow down the Mexican army as they retreated to San Antonio, which led to the battle's final outcome!

23. SABAL PALM SANCTUARY

Source: Loslazos

Why You Should Visit:

It is home to one of the last stands of old-growth Sabal Palm forest in the United States! If you like nature and beautiful sights, you'll love Sabal Palm Sanctuary. Because Sabal Palms almost completely surround it, the forest looks quite wild - like something out of a movie!

There are beautiful red and white oaks, palm fronds, and a variety of other trees in this area. You can also see outcroppings of limestone and beaver dams that have been used for more than 200 years by the local Seminole Indians. With so many beautiful sights to see, you won't mind going on a hike through this forest!

Location:

8435 Sabal Palm Grove Rd, Brownsville, TX 78521, USA

Best Time to Visit:

If you're planning to visit the sanctuary for a trip during the summer, be prepared for extremely hot temperatures. It can easily reach 100 degrees in this location in the summer! However, temperatures are uncommon to be this high on even a weeknight!

Pass/Permit/Fees:

There is no fee to enter Sabal Palm Sanctuary, but there are many fees associated with visiting their historic river plantation. An all-access pass costs $5 and allows entrance into both sites.

How to Get There:

The sanctuary is located close to Highway 83. Take Highway 83 South, turn left at Old Highway 281, go three miles, and turn right on Sabal Palm Grove Rd. From this point, it's two miles to the sanctuary.

GPS Coordinates:

25°51'10"N 97°25'03"W

Nearest Town/City:

The next-closest city is Tampico, Mexico. It is about 5 miles from the border.

Did You Know:

The term sabal palm comes from the Spanish word "sabal," meaning swamp or mud. Flora and fauna are an important part of this sanctuary, with more than 300 plant species present. The sanctuary is home to many different animals, including armadillos, coyotes, and even a few alligators!

24. TEXAS A&M BONFIRE MEMORIAL

Source: Patrick Creighton

Why You Should Visit:

If you have seen the old TV show, The Bachelor, you've probably seen an aerial view of Texas A&M University's Bonfire Memorial! American football teams call this area home during the fall and winter, and they mark their passing with an elaborate display of bonfires. This is one of the most popular destinations for visitors!

Just like how the TV show is filmed, the bonfire memorial takes about two days to build. This is because people bring logs of wood from all around Texas. These logs are then stacked, ring by ring, to form a bonfire that reaches up to 60 feet tall!

Location:

Texas A&M University, History Walk / Spirit Ring, College Station, TX 77843, United States

Best Time to Visit:

The best time to visit the university for this event is in the fall and winter, between September and March. It is not uncommon for temperatures to be below freezing during these months!

Pass/Permit/Fees:

There is no fee to enter Texas A&M's Bonfire Memorial, but there are several fees associated with visiting the university. The cost of a student's Hall Pass allows access to campus buildings, while an all-access pass costs $5. There are also fees associated with parking on campus, ranging from $10-$15, depending on the day!

How to Get There:

The university is situated within College Station, Texas. As you travel north on Texas Highway 6, turn left at the light onto College Station Pkwy, which leads to Texas A&M University. You will see signs for the Bonfire Memorial, but instead, turn right and follow the road around until it ends at a parking lot.

GPS Coordinates:
30.6227° N, 96.3352° W

Nearest City or Town:
The closest city is Bryan, which is about 10 miles away.

Did You Know:
The Bonfire Memorial was built in memories of Texas A&M students that had passed away during the creation of the original Bonfire. Over 90 students lost their lives during this construction, including 12 that died during the creation of Bonfire in 1999.

25. BRAZOS VALLEY VETERANS MEMORIAL

Why You Should Visit:

The Brazos Valley Veterans Memorial honors the men and women of the military who have fought in one way or another in Texas. This memorial is made up of two glass domes, each with its own theme. One dome is dedicated to Texas Military Forces, and the other to Texas State Military Forces. The display area also includes separate sections for Texas Rangers, Mexican War, Spanish-American War, and World War II. There is also a section for disabled veterans, which includes a special unit dedicated to the Veterans Airlift Command. As you walk around the memorial, you will see many names of both fallen soldiers and current military members. You can also visit their cemetery in the surrounding area for further inscriptions!

Location:

3101 Harvey Rd, College Station, TX 77845, United States

Best Time to Visit:

The best time to visit the memorial is between April and October, but you will be able to catch most of the display in any month!

Pass/Permit/Fees:

There is no fee to enter Brazos Valley Veterans Memorial. However, there are several fees associated with visiting the museum. If you plan on visiting the cemetery and viewing each section, there is a cost of $3 per person.

How to Get There:

To get there from College Station's city center, follow Harvey Rd or George Bush Dr south out of town until you get to Currey Ingram Rd. Follow this road until it ends at a parking lot for the memorial.

GPS Coordinates:

30.5655° N, 96.2484° W

Nearest City or Town:

The closest city is Bryan, which is about 10 miles south of College Station. The next closest town is Navasota, which is about 7 miles east of the Memorial on Highway 6.

Did You Know:

Brazos Valley Veterans Memorial was built in 2012 to honor soldiers that fought in military battles, including Desert Storm, Vietnam, and Operation Iraqi Freedom. Governor Rick Perry dedicated the memorial in December 2013!

26. CORPUS CHRISTI DOWNTOWN SEAWALL

Why You Should Visit:

Although Corpus Christi doesn't have a reputation for beaches and swimming, there is a local attraction in the city that is known for both of these. If you are interested in visiting a local attraction, the Seawall is worth checking out!

The Seawall extends for about six miles along the Texas Gulf Coast of Texas, so this coastline is well known for the beautiful sandy beach it is located on. The Seawall is also home to a number of shops, restaurants, and even hotels. If you're in town for a visit or business, you will surely enjoy your time here!

Location:

1590 N Shoreline Blvd, Corpus Christi, TX 78401-1100

Best Time to Visit:

The best time to visit this attraction is between April and October because this is when Corpus Christi's beaches are open year-round! Rain could delay the opening of the beaches from May until mid-June.

Pass/Permit/Fees:

There are no fees associated with Corpus Christi Downtown Seawall. However, there are several fees associated with visiting Corpus Christi. Most parking on downtown streets costs $1 per hour.

How to Get There:

To get to the Seawall, you can take I-37 to Shoreline Dr or Spinnaker Dr. Both of these streets are located on the beach side of Corpus Christi!

GPS Coordinates:

27° 48' 23.7816" N, 97° 23' 34.476" W.

Nearest City or Town:

The city of Corpus Christi is situated along the Gulf Coast in Texas. This city is about 220 miles from Houston, TX, and about 130 miles from San Antonio, TX.

Did You Know:

This seawall was created in 1985 to protect the city of Corpus Christi from flooding. The structure is built up of concrete blocks and is designed to withstand hurricane winds of up to 225 miles per hour! This area has become a popular attraction for tourists, as it is one of the few things that they can see during their visit that protects their money!

27. SOUTH TEXAS MUSIC WALK OF FAME

Why You Should Visit:

This attraction is a cool way to learn about country and pop music from Texas! As you stroll around the historic downtown district, you will hear tales about the artists and bands responsible for some of your favorite songs.

This attraction celebrates these musicians, including Selena Quintanilla, Willie Nelson, and George Strait. This attraction is worth checking out if you are a longtime music fan! It's a terrific opportunity to discover more about the musicians who have influenced your favorite music!

Location:

4250 S Alameda St, Corpus Christi, TX 78412, USA

Best Time to Visit:

The best time to visit the South Texas Music Walk of Fame is between April and September when the outdoor temperature averages around 55 degrees Fahrenheit.

Pass/Permit/Fees:

There are no fees associated with the South Texas Music Walk of Fame.

How to Get There:

To get to this attraction, take Highway 358/Shoreline Dr towards Corpus Christi Bay until it ends at Shoreline Mall in Corpus Christi. From there, continue walking along Shoreline Blvd until S Alameda St. From there; you will be able to find a map on the wall inside of J. Gilligan's Restaurant, which will show you the locations of each star.

GPS Coordinates:

30° 16' 21.81" N, 97° 44' 19.7808" W

Nearest City or Town:

This attraction is located in Corpus Christi, TX, which is about 130 miles away from San Antonio and 230 miles away from Houston.

Did You Know:

The Music Walk of Fame was created in 2000 by Beverly Brancaccio and Faye Payson in order to provide the public with an interactive way to learn about Texas-based music. The walk was originally anchored by a bronze plaque featuring Selena, Willie Nelson, and George Strait. The recognition of these artists helped promote Corpus Christi's music scene. Along with the replacement of old stars, there are more than seventy new ones for you to see!

28. MUSTANG ISLAND STATE PARK

Why You Should Visit:

Mustang Island State Park is a wonderful spot to escape the noise and chaos of daily life and unwind. The park is well-known for its beautiful beaches, which are great for swimming and sunbathing. It also offers plenty of activities that will keep you occupied while you're there: fishing, hiking trails, camping, hunting--you name it!

It is home to an incredible number of birds, including bald eagles and osprey. It's also known for its abundance of turtles, which makes it the perfect place for a hike or beach-goes-to-nature experience.

Location:

9394 State Highway 361, Corpus Christi, TX 78418

Best Time to Visit:

The best time to visit Mustang Island State Park is from May through October. Summer is the hottest season and may get too hot for you. But if you love the heat and want to enjoy a great beach destination, this is your best bet.

Pass/ Permit/ Fees:

There are no fees associated with Mustang Island State Park. However, there are a few fees that apply to visiting Corpus Christi. Most parking on downtown streets costs $1 per hour. Additionally, you will need to pay an entrance fee to enter the park. The entrance fee depends on your permit type but ranges from $5 to $10 per day.

How to Get There:

To get to the park, head to Corpus Christi and follow Highway 361 until you see Oso and Mustang Island State Park signs. Continue following the signs until you reach the covered pavilion.

GPS Coordinates:

N 27°40.519' W 97°10.616'

Nearest City or Town:

This park is located in Corpus Christi, TX. The closest city is Port Aransas, which is about 10 miles northeast of this park!

Did You Know:

The park was established in 1967 by Governor John Connally, who had visited the island in 1955 and found it "a paradise for birds." The park contains over 400 acres of forested wetlands and open areas of grassland with rare plants such as the Indian Paintbrush (Castilleja coronaria) and Texas Bluebonnet (Lupinus texensis).

29. WATERGARDENS FOUNTAINS

Why You Should Visit:

If you love fountains, Corpus Christi has some of the best in the world. You can walk through the gardens and see a variety of fountains--some are large and impressive, and others are smaller and less obvious. However, regardless of their size, they are all attractive.

To call it a fountain does not do it justice. The Bellagio-style water extravaganza encircles a large green area perfect for relaxing in the cooling spray and tranquil sound of rushing water. It's the perfect place to take a break from the midday heat or enjoy a romantic evening stroll.

Location:

1700 North Chaparral Street, Corpus Christi, TX 78401

Best Time to Visit:

The best time to visit Watergardens Fountains is from November through April when the temperature is cooler. If you want to see the fountains in action, go any time of the day and take a stroll around them.

Pass/ Permit/ Fees:

This area does require a parking pass for visitors. This pass can be purchased for $3 per person or $12 per vehicle.

How to Get There:

Take Highway 358/Shoreline Dr towards Corpus Christi Bay to get there. After it becomes Shoreline Blvd, continue following until you reach N Chaparral St. From there, continue straight until you see a sign that says "Watergardens." There will be plenty of parking available!

GPS Coordinates:

N 27° 39.53' W 97° 05.184'

Nearest City or Town:

This attraction is located in Corpus Christi, TX. The closest city is Port Aransas, which is about 10 miles northeast of this park!

Did You Know:

The water gardens were designed by Gustavo Soto, who also designed the San Antonio River Walk and other important public works projects in Texas. The fountains have been operational since 1999, so they're well-established now!

30. REUNION TOWER

Why You Should Visit:

Unrivaled views of the Dallas skyline and a truly unique experience.

You can expect this when you visit the Reunion Tower in Dallas, Texas. The tower has been an icon of the city for decades, but it's not just a tourist attraction—it's also one of the most fun ways to experience Dallas' artsy culture.

The Reunion Tower offers visitors some truly spectacular views of the city—especially once you've climbed up those stairs! You'll see everything from skyscrapers to lakes and gardens (hello, famous gardens!). And even if you don't want to take photos or do any sightseeing on your own time, you can still hang out at the bistro for a quick bite and glass of wine.

Location:

300 Reunion Blvd E, Dallas, TX 75207, United States

Best Time to Visit:

If you want to experience the city's best views, visit at night! It's definitely a sight to see at night.

Pass/ Permit/Fees:

An adult ticket costs $18, with discounts for children and seniors 65 and older.

How to Get There:

Take I-35E North towards Downtown Dallas (Exit 11), then take a right on Reunion Blvd. Drive until you reach a traffic light that is direct across from The Leonardo Hotel (a popular Westin Hotel). Turn right onto Reunion Blvd and keep driving straight until it splits into two roads. Take a left onto Reunion Blvd. Drive about two blocks and look for parking near the building.

GPS Coordinates:

32.7755° N, 96.8089° W

Nearest City or Town:

This attraction is located in Dallas, which is about 20 miles away from Fort Worth. The next closest city is Irving, which is about 10 miles away.

Did You Know:

The Reunion Tower (formerly known as the Reunion Center) was built as part of an effort to revitalize the city's downtown area in 1988 and was originally intended to be a performing arts center. The building has been undergoing renovations since 2010 and reopened as a museum in 2015.

31. BISHOP ARTS DISTRICT

Why You Should Visit:

The Bishop Arts District is unique compared to many other neighborhoods in Dallas since it has been constructed to resemble an old-fashioned main street. You'll find many of the buildings you'd see in the 'city across the tracks' in this area, but with a more modern theme—and it's all part of one large arts district!

There are lots of unique places to explore in Bishop Arts, including an art museum, botanical garden, brewery, candy shop, and so much more. And if you want to do some sightseeing while visiting the neighborhood? Just head over to one of the nearby attractions! There are plenty of options nearby (like The Bishop Arts District), so there's no need to spend your whole day out here.

Location:

Dallas, TX 75208, USA

Best Time to Visit:

Bishop Arts is a wonderful place to visit any time of the year, as it is a sheltered area away from the cold temperatures in the winter and the heat of summer. However, it especially offers a warmer, welcoming vibe during the spring and summer months.

Pass/ Permit/ Fees:

There are no admission fees to Bishop Arts, but parking is available on a first-come, first-served basis, and there is an hourly fee.

How to Get There:

From I-35E heading southbound, take Exit E (Bishop Ave). Turn right onto N Hall St before going over railroad tracks. The neighborhood will be on your right between 3rd and 5th Sts.

GPS Coordinates:

32.7473° N, 96.8304° W

Nearest City or Town:

Fort Worth is the next closest city, about 15 miles north of the neighborhood!

Did You Know:

If you've been to the movies, then you've probably seen a Texas Chainsaw Massacre shot in Dallas. You can see some of the locations used in the movie while visiting Bishop Arts and some of the movie's big props.

Bishop Arts were built with help from donations from community members and corporations, who funded the renovations and development of this arts district.

32. DALLAS ARBORETUM AND BOTANICAL GARDENS

Source: Michael Barera

Why You Should Visit:

Dallas Arboretum and Botanical Gardens are a must-see for anyone who loves nature and gardens. The gardens are located in the heart of downtown Dallas and feature many different types of plants and trees and a butterfly pavilion. The arboretum features over 12 acres of trees, including some rare varieties that are native to Texas.

The botanical gardens are home to more than 2000 different types of plants, which can be seen through windows on the ground level or from an elevated walkway. You'll find several ponds and fountains at the botanical gardens, which is one of the best parts—water features make everything look even prettier!

Location:

8525 Garland Rd, Dallas, TX 75218, United States

Best Time to Visit:

The best times to visit the gardens are in the spring and fall when they look their best. However, you can still see the gardens in winter, as long as you don't mind the cold!

Pass/ Permit/Fees:

The entrance fee is $7 for adults and $4 for children under 12 years old.

How to Get There:

From I-35, take Exit 160 and head east on N Buckner Blvd. Once you reach E Abrams Rd, turn left (towards the downtown area). You will be on Mockingbird Ln after it splits off from Abrams. Make a right onto N Macarthur Blvd, and then a second right onto W Mockingbird Ln. From that point on, follow the signs to the Dallas Arboretum and Botanical Gardens.

GPS Coordinates:

32.8236° N, 96.7166° W

Nearest City or Town:

The next closest city is Irving, which is about 15 miles away, while Fort Worth can be reached in approximately 20 minutes

Did You Know:

The Dallas Arboretum and Botanical Gardens was founded by Mrs. Mary Ellen Burns and was opened in 1988. The name of the gardens is inspired by Joseph C. Gores, who donated over $1 million to help turn this area into what it is today.

33. DEALEY PLAZA NATIONAL HISTORIC LANDMARK DISTRICT

Why You Should Visit:

When you visit Dealey Plaza, you'll find that it's actually a national historic landmark district, which is why the area is so popular with tourists. Former President John F. Kennedy was shot in the back and died from his wounds, exactly where the plaza is now. The former.

The architecture of Dealey Plaza is quite unique compared to other places in Dallas. It's mostly made of warehouses from the early 20th century that is now used for various museums and shops in downtown Dallas, making it unique.

Location:

500 Main St, Dallas, TX 75202-3521

Best Time to Visit:

Spring and autumn are the most lovely seasons; therefore, these are the finest times to visit Dealey Plaza. However, you can still see Dealey Plaza in the winter if it's not too cold!

Pass/ Permit/ Fees:

There is no admission fee to visit Dealey Plaza, but there is a $5 parking fee. But you can also park for free at the Strand Theater parking lot.

How to Get There:

From I-45 Northbound to I-45 Southbound, take Exit 37B (Depot St). Once you've exited from the freeway, turn left onto N Main St and then left again (on your first right) onto E Houston St. You'll be on N Houston St after that. From there, follow the signs to the Dealey Plaza Visitor Information Center.

GPS Coordinates:

32° 46.745′ N, 96° 48.525′ W

Nearest City or Town:

Fort Worth is the next closest city, about 15 miles away.

Did You Know:

The plaza is home to the JFK Memorial, where President Kennedy's eternal flame burns. The concrete slab at the foot of this memorial is known as "the Grassy Knoll." It's a reference to a hunting term for where an animal is wounded and lies.

34. THE DALLAS WORLD AQUARIUM

Source: Jay R Simonson Jsim01

Why You Should Visit:

The Dallas World Aquarium is an excellent destination for families with children of all ages, as it offers something for everyone. The aquarium features over 400 different species of animals from around the world! Some of the animals on display include sharks, penguins, otters, reptiles, and even birds, such as flamingos and toucans.

In addition to the animal exhibits, you'll also find a tropical rainforest area full of exotic plants and animals, a giant tank of stingrays, and a butterfly pavilion where you can learn about butterflies and watch them fly around their habitat. An underwater tunnel lets you get up close to fish and sharks! The Dallas World Aquarium is truly an educational experience for visitors of all ages.

Location:

1801 N Griffin St, Dallas, TX 75202, United States

Best Time to Visit:

The best time to visit the Dallas World Aquarium is in the spring and fall months when it's warm outside but not too rainy.

Pass/ Permit/ Fees:

Admission starts at $18.95 for children ages three to 12 and $26.95 for adults.

How to Get There:

From I-20, head north on Marsalis Ave. From I-35, take Exit 330B and go east on Boat Club Rd. Then, turn left onto E Colorado Blvd and finally a left onto Griffin St. The aquarium will be on your left after you make a left onto Houston St.

GPS Coordinates:

32.7835° N, 96.8054° W

Nearest City or Town:

The next closest city aside from Dallas is Fort Worth, which is about 15 miles away, while Denton and Arlington are about 60 miles away.

Did You Know:

The aquarium opened its doors in 1985 and was the first major marine life facility in Texas. It is currently one of the most frequented locations in Dallas.

35. DALLAS ZOO

Why You Should Visit:

The Dallas Zoo is the perfect place to visit if you're looking to get up close and personal with some of our favorite animals! The zoo features over 2,000 animals that call this zoo home, including several rare species. The zoo covers 74 acres of land and has plenty of areas with trees and plants for visitors to enjoy while they are walking around, too.

All of the animals here are treated with the care that they deserve. The zoo follows a naturalistic approach, which means that they create environments as similar to what you would find in the wild as possible. The Dallas Zoo is one of the largest zoos in America, and it's certainly worth visiting!

Location:

650 S R L Thornton Fwy, Dallas, TX 75203, United States

Best Time to Visit:

The best time to visit the Dallas Zoo is the spring and fall months, as that is when most of the animals are outside and more photogenic. But if you're looking for some shade while you're at the zoo, there's a nice area in front of the giraffes and elephants with lots of trees!

Pass/ Permit/ Fees:

Under 2 years old is free of charge, while those that are over 2 and up are $8. The parking fee is $10 per vehicle, while a 2-day pass is $26 and can be purchased at the gate of the zoo.

How to Get There:

The Dallas Zoo is located at 650 S. R. L. Thornton Fwy and is just off I-35E in Far North Dallas, about 20 minutes from downtown Dallas by car. From I-20, head south on Marsalis Ave, then head west on Blackland Rd for about 1/2 mile until you see the sign for the zoo on your right-hand side. From I-35 E, go northbound, exit onto Royal Lane, turn left toward N R L Thornton Fwy, and follow the signs to the zoo.

GPS Coordinates:

32.7405° N, 96.8162° W

Nearest City or Town:

The next closest city is Fort Worth, about 25 miles away. Denton and Arlington are about 60 miles away.

Did You Know:

The Dallas Zoo started as a drive-through safari exhibit in 1907, but it wasn't until 1934 that the current zoo structure took form and was able to hold a variety of animals, including bison and other large species.

36. DALLAS CATTLE DRIVE SCULPTURES

Why You Should Visit:

The Dallas Cattle Drive Sculptures are an interesting sight to see in Dallas. They house bronze sculptures that depict cowboys driving cattle through the west Texas plains. The artwork is spread over 1,426 acres of land, and a few museums and monuments are also located on the property.

The artwork is really unique, so it's worth checking out if you're ever in the Dallas area! This area is just south of I-20, about a 15-minute drive from downtown Dallas.

Location:

1428 Young St, Dallas, TX 75202, USA

Best Time to Visit:

The best time to visit the Cattle Drive Sculptures is the spring and fall months, as the area has plenty of trees and other vegetation to make the scenery look a lot more pleasant.

Pass/ Permit/ Fees:

No admission fee is required for this attraction in Dallas. How to Get There:

The Dallas Cattle Drive Sculptures are just off Interstate 20, and you can get there by taking Exit 280. Take a left onto N Cockrell Hill Rd, then a right onto W Jefferson Blvd. Continue north on Jefferson until you see the sculpture area on your left.

GPS Coordinates:

32°46'35"N, 96°48'05"W

Nearest City or Town:

The next closest city is Tyler, about 45 miles away. Denton and Arlington are about 60 miles away.

Did You Know:

The artwork is named after the Emmett Lee Cattle Company, which used to own the land that it is on. It was first conceived in 1894 and was completed in 1915. The artwork represents a herd of cattle being driven west, away from homesteading settlements, into the wide-open grasslands of Texas.

37. FOUNTAIN PLACE

Why You Should Visit:

Located in Dallas, Texas, Fountain Place is a beautiful botanical garden and water park that's just minutes from downtown Dallas. The park is like an oasis in the middle of the city. It is full of lush plants and tall trees that provide shade from the hot sun as you walk along its many paths. You can spend hours exploring different parts of this park—there are several waterfalls, pools, and even an amphitheater! If it's too hot for you to enjoy the water features, you can always cool off by taking a dip in one of its two rivers or lakes.

The whole experience makes for an ideal day trip for families with children or friends who want to explore new places together. Fountain Place is ideal if you want to escape the hustle and bustle of Dallas life!

Location:

1445 Ross Ave Suite 5100, Dallas, TX 75202-2711

Best Time to Visit:

The park is open 24 hours but will be closed during winter months due to extreme cold and snow. The ideal season for visiting the park in spring and summer, as the weather will be warm enough for you to enjoy the many water features while they're still open.

Pass/ Permit/ Fees:

1-hour costs around $4.00, while 24 hours cost approximately $14.00.

How to Get There:

Fountain Place is easily accessible by public transportation, and it's only a short walk away from Downtown Dallas and the West End District. You can reach the park using bus route 459 or 461, both of which stop at Ross Avenue & Houston Street near the main entrance of Fountain Place. The park is also accessible via the DART Rail Line, which stops at Union Station near the two sides of Fountain Place and is served by the Red and Blue Line. For more information and to plan your route, check out this interactive map.

GPS Coordinates:

32.7848° N, 96.8025° W

Nearest City or Town:

Plano, Garland, and Irving are about 30-45 minutes away by car.

Did You Know:

Fountain Place was first opened in 1987 and underwent a renovation in 2008. Brookfield Properties now own Fountain Place, and an interesting fact about the company is that it also owns such buildings as the Sears Tower in Chicago and Manhattan's World Financial Center.

38. WHITE ROCK LAKE

Source: Luis Tamayo

Why You Should Visit:

White Rock Lake is a classic Dallas attraction located north of the city. The lake covers about 1,200 acres and is home to many different types of wildlife, including ducks, geese, cranes, beavers, and alligators. This lake is on the Audubon Society's list of top 100 birdwatching spots in the United States! It's also a great place to enjoy nature and go for a scenic trail walk or run. Several trails are available around the lake (the longest being just over 6 miles long), so you can enjoy a relaxing day without driving too far or running into traffic jams.

If you are planning on visiting White Rock Lake, be sure to visit the Audubon Center at Greenways Park, located right next to the lake; it offers fascinating exhibits and attractions about birds and other wildlife. The center also runs bird-watching workshops and talks where you can learn about the different types of birds you might spot while on one of their many walks.

Location:

542 E. Jefferson Blvd. Dallas, Texas 75203

Best Time to Visit:

The best time to visit White Rock Lake is during the summer when the weather is cooler, and you can enjoy the area without worrying as much about the heat. If you're planning a trip in the winter months, check with the park before setting off.

Pass/ Permit/ Fees:

No Admission Fee - No parking fee is charged for vehicle use at White Rock Lake Park. If you wish to park in one of the public parking lots near White Rock Lake, you can anticipate paying approximately $3.00 per hour or $15.00 per day.

How to Get There:

The park is located just north of downtown Dallas on the White Rock Lake Loop Road. It's easy to get to, so you can either travel there by car or use public transportation. If you have a bike, you can easily make your way there by following the directions on this map. You can also reach this park by taking bus route 458 and getting off at Morrow Road and Lake Ray Hubbard.

GPS Coordinates:
32.8281° N, 96.7253° W

Nearest City or Town:
The next town aside from Dallas is Irving, Texas (about 13.4 miles away).

Did You Know:
This park was originally built in 1900 and is one of the first urban parks of its kind. The park was once used for military training purposes, but it fell into disrepair and was officially closed in 2000. In 2007, a comprehensive renovation project began, bringing new life to the old park. There are now beautiful gardens and several trails to explore.

39. TRINITY GROVES

Why You Should Visit:

Trinity Groves is a Dallas neighborhood that is home to some of the city's oldest, most prestigious homes. Known for its grandeur and history, it has been a destination for the high society for over 100 years.

The Trinity Groves neighborhood is located just south of downtown Dallas, close to Oak Lawn and the Arts District. It is popular for its streets lined with trees, which make it simple to travel by bike or foot. It also has plenty of restaurants, bars, and cafes catering to the neighborhood's residents and visitors. If you're looking for an area close to the city center in which you can relax and enjoy all that Dallas has to offer, this is the place for you!

Location:

331 Singleton Blvd Suite 200, Dallas, TX 75212, USA

Best Time to Visit:

The best time to go is in the summer when it's cooler, and there are more things to do. If you're planning a trip during winter months, check with the park before setting off.

Pass / Permit / Fees:

No fees are charged for Trinity Groves since it's technically considered a private area. However, some stores and restaurants within the neighborhood may charge a small fee for parking.

How to Get There:

There are several ways to get to Trinity Groves, depending on your preferred mode of transport and desired route. You can travel directly via Singleton Boulevard through the neighborhood if you're traveling by car. For public transportation options, look at DART. The nearest train stations that give access to Trinity Groves are the Pearl/Arts District Station in downtown Dallas and JOYA Station in Oak Cliff.

GPS Coordinates:

32.7782° N, 96.8291° W

How to Get There:

Public transportation has yet to reach the area, so if you're planning to visit, be sure to drive there or use a designated ride-sharing service. You can reach the Trinity Groves neighborhood via highway 75 or 175. Also, make sure to give yourself plenty of time while driving to and from the park, so you don't get stuck in traffic jams around town.

GPS Coordinates:

32.7782° N, 96.8291° W

Nearest City or Town:

The nearest town to the Trinity Groves neighborhood is Oak Cliff, which is 7.2 miles away. Downtown Dallas is 9.7 miles away, and the Arts District is 10.5 miles away from the park itself.

Did You Know:

The history of Trinity Groves can be traced back to 1857, when the first African American settlement in Dallas was established along South Martin Luther King Boulevard between Bryan Street and Lamar Street. The community grew quickly; by 1879, more than 100 families lived there. By 1890, the area had become so popular that it was incorporated into a town called South Dallas.

40. GIANT EYEBALL

Why You Should Visit:

If you're a fan of scary movies and like to live life to the fullest, check out the giant eyeball in Dallas. How does it compare to other spooky sites like the Haunted Mansion in Disneyland? It's definitely a contender for the most terrifyingly awesome spot in town!

Location:

1601 Main St, Dallas, TX 75201, United States

Best Time to Visit:

If you're planning a trip to the giant eyeball in Dallas, be sure to visit during the day, when it will be easier to see and photograph.

Pass/Permit/Fees:

No admission fee is charged for this attraction - parking fees may apply.

How to Get There:

The park is located just north of downtown Dallas on the White Rock Lake Loop Road. It's easy to get to, so you can either travel there by car or use public transportation. You can also reach this park by taking bus route 458 and getting off at Morrow Road and Lake Ray Hubbard.

GPS Coordinates:

32.7814° N, 96.7983° W

Nearest City or Town:

The closest town away from the giant eyeball is Downtown Dallas, which is 1.5 miles away. The area around the park is known as White Rock Lake Loop, and it's easily accessible by car or on foot.

Did You Know:

The Giant Eyeball in Dallas is actually the second eyeball structure built by artist Claes Oldenburg. The first one was back in 1974, near Houston, and it was shaped like a shoe instead of an eye. It's made of concrete, steel, and fiberglass and weighs about 25 tons.

41. HALL OF STATE

Why You Should Visit:

This building is a testament to the history of the state of Texas! You'll get to travel through time in terms of Texan history and art here.

The Hall of State is among the fascinating museums you will ever visit. It's in a historic building and has a lot of cool historical items from Texas.

You'll see things like a replica of Sam Houston's cabin and one of the original copies of the Declaration of Independence, along with more recent artifacts like items from NASA missions! The Hall of State is a great place to learn about the history of Texas in a fun way.

Location:

3939 Grand Ave, Dallas, TX 75210, United States

Best Time to Visit:

The museum offers a fun, educational atmosphere all year round, especially during the spring and summer months. The museum has an outdoor area to enjoy during warmer weather, too!

Pass/ Permit/ Fees:

Admission fees start at $6 for children aged three to 12 and $8 for adults aged 13 years old and up. Children under three are admitted free of charge.

How to Get There:

The closest major roadway to the museum is Interstate 35E (exit Grand Avenue), which can be reached from I-35E by taking Exit 196A onto Interstate 30 West towards downtown Dallas (Merge onto Grand Ave), or from U.S. 75 North, take Exit 308 and follow the signs to Interstate 35E South.

GPS Coordinates:

32.7807° N, 96.7610° W

Nearest City or Town:

The next major city aside from Dallas is Fort Worth, which is about 25 miles away from the museum.

Did You Know:

President John F. Kennedy gave his famous "City of Hate" speech from the rear platform of a train car in this building when he was in Dallas on November 22, 1963—50 years later; the museum commemorated the event with a special exhibit to highlight this moment.

42. THANKS-GIVING SQUARE

Source: Joe Mabel

Why You Should Visit:

Thanks-Giving Square is a popular park in the area of downtown Dallas that offers visitors a chance to escape the city buzz while still enjoying all it has to offer. The square features a beautiful fountain, lush gardens, free water fountains, and an abundance of birds and butterflies throughout the area. It is one of the most popular parks in Dallas, both among tourists and locals.

Thanks-Giving Square is the largest public park in downtown Dallas and a place where residents, workers, and visitors alike can relax, enjoy the city's beauty, or relax with their friends.

Location:

1627 Pacific Ave, Dallas, TX 75201, United States

Best Time to Visit:

Thanks- Giving Square is a great place to visit year-round, but the best time to go is in early spring when the park's flowers and plants are in full bloom. From mid-October to February, you can enjoy the warm weather and colder nights that are ideal for visiting a place like this.

Pass / Permit / Fees:

There are no fees associated with Thanks-Giving Square. The only cost you'll have to pay is for parking your car.

How to Get There:

You can get there by car by traveling along St. Paul St to Pacific Avenue, but it's better to drive via Interstate 35E, exit Elm Street, and head north along Commerce Street. The nearest train station is Union Station (about 8 blocks away). For bus routes, check out this interactive Google map.

GPS Coordinates:

32.7830° N, 96.7982° W

Nearest City or Town:

The immediate residential areas include Fair Park, Old East Dallas, and Deep Ellum, which is about 3 miles away from Thanks-Giving Square.

Did You Know:

Thanks-Giving Square was originally commissioned by President William McKinley in 1896 and built for Thanksgiving Day in 1899. It was designed by architect Frederick Louis Hutton, who also designed the Mercantile National Bank Building and the Hall of State in Oklahoma City, Oklahoma.

43. NASHER SCULPTURE CENTER

Why You Should Visit:

It is pretty much the same as combining art and architecture. The Nasher Sculpture Center offers sculpture, art, and architecture enthusiasts alike a chance to enjoy some of the finest works by some of the best sculptors in the country while also providing some great views of the city.

The Nasher Sculpture Center's newest exhibition, "Art in the Garden: Invention and Imagination in the Garden," features sculptures by Charles Ray, David Adjaye, Daniel Libeskind, and many others. This exhibition features work created using plants, natural materials, and parts of trees as its source material.

Location:

2001 Flora St, Dallas, TX 75201, United States

Best Time to Visit:

The best time to visit the Nasher Sculpture Center is any day between April and November when it's warm enough to enjoy the outside area. If you're more interested in seeing the inside exhibits, then it's best to visit between October and March—it'll still be nice outside, so that you can enjoy the views from there. Otherwise, you might want to visit during December when the center is decorated for Christmas!

Pass / Permit / Fees:

There are no fees associated with visiting Nasher Sculpture Center, but they do encourage visitors to get a subscription to their email list so they can get access to special offers and events.

How to Get There:

If you're driving from downtown, head over Highland Park Boulevard towards Stemmons Freeway, take the exit for LBJ Freeway/Sam Rayburn Tollway, and then go north on LBJ Freeway to Flora Street. The sculpture center is located a little more than two miles north of Flora Street at 2001 Flora Street, Dallas, TX.

GPS Coordinates:

32° 47' 10.19" N, -96° 48' 0.29" W

Nearest City or Town:

The closest city to the sculpture center is Dallas, about 2.5 miles away. Irving is the next closest city, about 5 miles from the center.

Did You Know:

The Nasher Sculpture Center was founded in 1986 when it became the first art center in the Metroplex. There are more than 175 sculptures in the museum's collection, including works by Rodin, Degas, Rothko, and Robert Indiana.

44. GRAPEVINE VINTAGE RAILROAD

Source: Stefan Bethke

Why You Should Visit:

Have you ever dreamed of seeing a miniature train that travels around the countryside? Then you'll want to make sure you head to Grapevine Vintage Railroad.

Grapevine Vintage Railroad offers an up-close view of a historical reproduction of the earliest kind of railroad cars used in America, by the way! The steam engine that runs the train is one of twelve such engines still running in America today, and also features original equipment as well as newly commissioned operable replica operating equipment. The railroad has its origin in Garland, Texas, and is one of only three operating railroads with this type of locomotive.

Location:

707 S Main St, Grapevine, TX 76051, United States

Best Time to Visit:

The best times to go to Grapevine Vintage Railroad are from May through October, as the days get longer and the train runs at night seven days a week.

Pass / Permit / Fees:

The cost of riding on a train is $5 per person or $5 per vehicle with up to 8 people in it. Children under five years old ride free of charge if an adult accompanies them. There are also no minimum age requirements for riding!

How to Get There:

Grapevine Vintage Railroad is located one mile north of I-30 on I-635—take Exit 344A towards Highway 377/Main Street, North, and then follow the signs to Main Street. It is also about 20 minutes from DFW Airport, or take I-635 to Grapevine Highway, turn right onto Main Street, and go 2.5 miles to the railroad station.

GPS Coordinates:

32° 57' 57.5748" N and 97° 2' 33.936" W

Nearest City or Town:

Irving is the closest city, about 8 miles from the railroad station. Nearby cities, including Plano, Cedar Hill, and Richardson, are within a 30-minute drive from the train station. The nearest town is Grapevine—about .5 miles away from the railroad station.

Did You Know:

Grapevine Vintage Railroad has a rich history that dates back to the 1940s. It was purchased in 1988 by the Shafner family, who helped rebuild the entire railroad with new equipment and operating equipment, including the restoration of several locomotives.

45. DEVILS RIVER STATE NATURAL AREA

Why You Should Visit:

Those looking for a rugged wilderness experience in Texas should consider visiting Devils River State Natural Area. This area is perfect for lovers of hiking and camping, as it features extensive trails through dense woods and unspoiled natural beauty throughout the state park.

The river that the area is named after is home to alligators, so you'll want to be vigilant in your search for them. However, you can also enjoy canoeing, fishing, and swimming on the water, which is a great way to relax during your visit. The scenery here is beautiful and peaceful, so it's perfect for an afternoon or weekend retreat!

Location:

21715 Dolan Crk Rd, Del Rio, TX 78840, United States

Best Time to Visit:

The best times to visit this area are spring and summer. The weather is cooler during these periods, plus you'll enjoy more daylight hours.

Pass/ Permit/ Fees:

If you want to access the Devils River State Natural Area, you need a Devils River Access Permit (DRAP). The price of DRAP is $10 per person per day. The area is open from April to October and has limited parking spots.

How to Get There:

From I-10 heading northbound, take Exit 234 (Dolan Creek Rd) and drive about 20 miles. Turn right at the light onto Dolan Creek Rd and follow it for about nine miles.

GPS Coordinates:

29.9402° N, 100.9698° W

Nearest City or Town:

Aside from Del Rio, about 25 miles east of Devils River State Natural Area, the next closest cities are San Antonio, TX, and Corpus Christi, TX, which are about 100 miles away.

Did You Know:

This 37,000-acre state natural area has rocky canyons made of limestone and is one of the rivers in Texas with the best ecosystem.

46. DOLAN FALLS

Source: Clinton & Charles Robertson from RAF Lakenheath, UK & San Marcos, TX, USA & UK

Why You Should Visit:

If you ever visit the Devils River State Natural Area, you can also see this waterfall is located in the area. This waterfall is one of the most beautiful in the state, and it's a great place to snap a few pictures while enjoying the scenery.

You can also see a trail built along the top of the waterfall so that visitors can see it from above. You'll find several campgrounds and cabins nearby as well. So even if you're only passing through for an afternoon, you can easily spend a day or two in this area before continuing your road trip!

Location:

21715 Dolan Creek Rd. Del Rio, TX 78840.

Best Time to Visit:

The best times to visit this area are spring and summer. The weather will be mild during these periods, with plenty of sunshine and blue skies.

Pass/ Permit/ Fees:

If you want to access the Devils River State Natural Area, you need a Devils River Access Permit (DRAP). The price of DRAP is $10 per person per day.

How to Get There:

From the Devils River State Natural Area entrance, take the trail that leads to the waterfall.

GPS Coordinates:

29°53' N, 101°00' W

Nearest City or Town:

Aside from Del Rio, which is about 25 miles east of Devils River State Natural Area, the next closest cities are San Antonio, TX, and Corpus Christi, TX, which are about 100 miles away.

Did You Know:

The falls are named after James A. Dolan, who owned the land where the waterfall is located.

47. LAKE AMISTAD NATIONAL RECREATION AREA

Why You Should Visit:

You will find a better place to enjoy a scenic lake for swimming and fishing than Lake Amistad National Recreation Area. In addition to the many activities on or around the lake (like fishing, kayaking, and swimming), you can also enjoy boat tours, picnicking, and other outdoor adventures.

Location:

4121 Veterans Boulevard, Del Rio, TX 78840

Best Time to Visit:

Most people go in the summer because it is warm and dry. You can also enjoy year-round lake activities, but avoiding the coldest and wettest parts of winter is best.

Pass/ Permit/ Fees:

Since the dam is an official Port-of-Entry, everyone who wants to get into the lake must have a valid passport with them.

How to Get There:

From I-10 heading northbound, take Exit 226. Turn right at the light onto Veterans Blvd and drive about five miles. It would help if you turned left onto a small gravel road called Hwy 77. Follow this road over a bridge and continue past the park headquarters until you reach the National Parks Service office entrance on your right side (about one mile).

GPS Coordinates:

29°26'12"N 101°3'0"W

Nearest City or Town:

Del Rio is about 40 miles east of Lake Amistad National Recreation Area. The next closest city is San Antonio, about 135 miles away!

Did You Know:

Lake Amistad National Recreation Area is a massive international reservoir renowned for its crystal-clear water and stunning scenery. It was originally named "Las Lajas Reservoir" when it was first built. The name was changed to Lake Amistad in 1970, which is Spanish for "the stranded one."

48. CHAMIZAL NATIONAL MEMORIAL

Why You Should Visit:

You'll be able to experience an important part of U.S. history on this bit of land! After a dispute between Mexico and the U.S., this memorial was built as a symbol of peace and cooperation between the two nations. You'll see how it was made in an exhibition area at the national memorial, where you can see its construction from different points of view.

Location:

800 S San Marcial St, El Paso, TX 79905, USA

Best Time to Visit:

This location is best to visit during the winter because the weather will be pleasant, and there will be fewer people than at other times of the year.

Pass/Permit/Fees:

Chamizal National Memorial does not charge to get into the park, use its facilities, or attend events put on by the park.

How to Get There:

Take I-10 heading eastbound and take Exit 15, which is San Marcial St. Follow the signs towards El Paso Chamizal National Memorial until you arrive at your destination.

GPS Coordinates:

31°46'4"N 106°27'15"W

Nearest City or Town:

Aside from El Paso, about 50 miles, the next closest cities are Houston, TX, and Dallas, TX, which are about 125 miles away.

Did You Know:

The site is named in honor of Chico (Charles) A. R. Garza, who visited the United States as a student while attending college in El Paso and decided to honor his heritage by building a monument to mark the Chamizal dispute. He believed this would be a good place to start future cooperation between Mexicans and Anglo-Americans. Mr. Garza died on July 17, 1964, of an assassination attempt while visiting Houston, celebrating his wife's birthday with family members and friends.

49. MAGOFFIN HOME STATE HISTORIC SITE

Why You Should Visit:

Magoffin is a uniquely historic site, as it was the site of a small community in El Paso that Irish immigrants built. The Magoffin family began building the area in 1855, and their houses were built around an 1875 cemetery. Today, you can see some of these historical structures and explore the entire Magoffin community area.

Location:

1120 Magoffin Ave, El Paso, TX 79901, United States

Best Time to Visit:

Spring is the best time to visit this historic site for obvious reasons. The trees are blooming, and there's also a lot of other beautiful plant life to enjoy in springtime. Fall is a good time to visit because it's generally a bit cooler, and the foliage will still be changing.

Pass/Permit/Fees:

The cost is $4 per person for groups of 10 or more and $3 per person for individuals.

How to Get There:

Take I-10 North and take Exit 162, which is Magoffin Avenue (perpendicular to I-10). Go through the traffic light, turn left onto Magoffin Street, and go one block. Follow the signs to enter into Magoffin State Historic Site.

GPS Coordinates:

31°45'45"N, 106°28'37"W

Nearest City or Town:

Aside from El Paso, the closest city is Albuquerque, NM, which is about 200 miles away.

Did You Know:

Magoffin was founded by Irish immigrants and is known to be a small community built around a cemetery. The area was named after Thomas Magoffin, a state senator from Kentucky who founded the El Paso Company in 1853. The company operated as an Irish business for several years, making it possible for many Irish immigrants to come to El Paso.

50. OLD FORT BLISS REPLICA

Source: PsyDor

Why You Should Visit:

Avid history buffs will love this recreation area, which is a replica of the Old Fort Bliss and the old U.S. Army post in El Paso, Texas. You'll get a chance to explore this impressive structure and learn about military history by viewing a couple of outdoor exhibits that tell the story of Fort Bliss.

Location:

5054 Pershing Rd, El Paso, TX 79925, United States

Best Time to Visit:

Spring is the best time to visit this site since you'll be able to see all of the outdoor displays at their peak. Summer is also fun because they will have a staff member on duty in front of the museum to answer questions.

Pass/ Permit/ Fees:

You'll need a special Fort Bliss Pass ($25 for adults, $10 for children under 18) if you plan on visiting the post and museum.

How to Get There:

When you arrive at the Old Fort Bliss, follow signs for Ft Bliss RV Park and Park Headquarters parking lot. Find parking in this area, walk through gate M1 onto Pershing Road (the first road past gate M1), and take a left for the museum.

GPS Coordinates:

31.8000° N, 106.4267° W

Nearest City or Town:

Aside from El Paso, the closest city is Las Cruces, which is about 100 miles away.

Did You Know:

This post is believed to be the oldest standing military post in the U.S. It was used as a Civil War training site, and it was here that Theodore Roosevelt served his required two years of service before becoming a colonel and advancing to the rank of major general during World War I.

51. HUECO TANKS STATE HISTORIC SITE

Why You Should Visit:

Hueco Tanks is a state historic site with a national reputation for its primitive and historic rock art. You can explore seven giant natural rock shelters, each of which has spectacular and unique artwork from the Native Americans who inhabited this area.

Location:

6900 Hueco Tanks Road No. 1, El Paso, TX 79938, United States

Best Time to Visit:

Spring is the best time to visit this park since you can see all the beautiful wildflowers in bloom. Fall is pretty nice, too, since it's drier and warmer than spring. Summer can be hot and humid here, so during that time; it's best to visit during the early morning hours or towards the evening.

Pass/Permit/Fees:

Tours are $2 per person, ages 5 and up, and children 4 and under are free

How to Get There:

From I-10, exit at YO Ranch Road. Make a right on San Antonio Avenue, and go west for about two miles until you cross Hueco Tanks Road. Turn left and gogo about two miles more, and you'll see the Hueco Tanks State Historic Site entrance.

GPS Coordinates:

31° 54' 58.932" N, 106° 2' 36.402" W

Nearest City or Town:

Aside from El Paso, the closest city is San Antonio, which is about 14 miles away.

Did You Know:

Hueco Tanks is a former sacred site for the Indians, who came from hundreds of miles away to what was once a watering hole for the herds of buffalo and other animals that roamed this area. It's also one of the few places where you can find petroglyphs that date back to 8,000 years ago.

52. MCDONALD OBSERVATORY

Why You Should Visit:

You can see the stars in all their glory here at the McDonald Observatory, and you can visit the various planetariums and science exhibits that are located in the observatory's visitors center.

Location:

McDonald Observatory, 3640 Dark Sky Dr, Fort Davis, TX 79734, United States

Best Time to Visit:

You'll need to get here before sunset if you want to catch all of the displays and presentations. Visitors go on the hour, so it's a good idea to drive or take a tour early in the day and plan on staying until after dusk.

Pass/Permit/Fees:

A general admission ticket is $3. Guided tours are $10 for adults and $5 for children under 5 years old.

How to Get There:

From I-10, exit at Fort Davis-Shafter Road (TX 118). Go west for about 28 miles, and you'll see the observatory's entrance on the left side of the road.

GPS Coordinates:

30.6797° N, 104.0247° W

Nearest City or Town:

Aside from Fort Davis, the closest city, the next biggest nearby town is Alpine, about 41 miles away.

Did You Know:

The McDonald Observatory is home to a variety of telescopes and other equipment that enable astronomers to observe and discover more about space. The International Dark-Sky Association designated this observatory as a Dark Sky Park—the only one in Texas to receive the distinction!

53. CHIHUAHUAN DESERT NATURE CENTER

Why You Should Visit:

If you're interested in seeing a wide range of desert wildlife and plants, check out the Chihuahuan Desert Nature Center. The natural exhibits here are very diverse, and they get plenty of use from El Pasoans looking to escape the heat. There's also a nice selection of interesting educational displays on topics like animal adaptations, desert survival, and plant life.

Location:

43869 TX-118, Fort Davis, TX 79734, USA

Best Time to Visit:

Year-round, spring is a great time to visit since most of the plants and animals bloom. Fall is usually a good time, too, as it's cooler, and there is more foliage changing colors. Of course, summer can also be beautiful with lots of wildflowers.

Pass/Permit/Fees:

$6.50 for adults. Children 12 and under are free.

How to Get There:

From I-10, take exit 48, go west on TX-118 (signs will direct you which direction), and drive west to the crossroads. Turn right and drive a mile until you come to a junction. Take the left fork, which will lead you to the nature center.

GPS Coordinates:

30.5416° N, 103.8393° W

Nearest City or Town:

The next nearest town is Post, about 48 miles away. El Paso is about 60 miles to the east, and Ciudad Juarez is about 80 miles to the west.

Did You Know:

The Chihuahuan Desert Nature Center is a Southwestern Association for Biological Diversity project and the Nature Conservancy project. Its goal is to preserve this important desert ecosystem, which humans and various other animals once inhabited. Today, you can see various plants and animals, including coyotes, bobcats, javelinas, ocelots, desert bighorn sheep, and the rare black-tailed jackrabbits.

54. DAVIS MOUNTAIN STATE PARK

Why You Should Visit:

Davis Mountain State Park offers a lot of amenities for its visitors, including an impressive hiking trail and camping facilities. It is also one of the only places in the region where you can see a 300-year-old oak tree!

Location:

TX-118, Fort Davis, TX 79734, USA

Best Time to Visit:

Year-round. Though it is situated in an arid region and often very hot during summer, the park has shaded picnic areas that make it a great place to stop for a break. Spring and fall are also nice times to visit because all the flowers bloom.

Pass/Permit/Fees:

Free for children under 12 years of age; $6.50 for adults (day use only)

How to Get There:

From I-10, take exit 48, go west on TX-118 (signs will direct you which direction), and drive west to the crossroads. Turn right and drive a mile until you come to a junction. Take the left fork, which will lead you to the park's entrance.

GPS Coordinates:

30.599103° N, 103.929450° W

Nearest City or Town:

The closest city is Fort Davis, around 7 miles away! Ciudad Juarez is about 80 miles across the border from this park.

Did You Know:

Davis Mountain State Park is a Southwestern Association for Biological Diversity project and the Nature Conservancy project. Its goal is to preserve this important desert ecosystem, which humans and various other animals once inhabited. Today, you can see the remains of the last Indian village, the O'Odham Indian Village. This archaeological site was discovered in 2004 and contained remains from ancient cultures that primarily used this area for hunting and planting crops. Meteor Crater is about 18 miles away from this park and can be seen in the distance if you're walking around on the boulders that line this beautiful state park!

55. FORT DAVIS NATIONAL HISTORIC SITE

Why You Should Visit:

The US Army Corps of Engineers was involved in building Fort Davis and other military outposts in the area during the 19th century. To preserve this historic military site, the National Park Service decided to purchase it and convert it into a national park. Now, visitors can explore the history of this region, learn about its connections to Native Americans, and enjoy spectacular views from the top of Davis Mountain.

Location:

1504 State St, Fort Davis, TX 79734, USA

Best Time to Visit:

Year-round. Due to the wide variety of plant and animal species that reside here, the best times to visit are spring, summer, and fall. However, winter can be pleasant if you wish to escape the heat.

Pass/Permit/Fees:

Commercial groups are charged $10.00 per person aged 16 and older. Educational groups may request a fee waiver in writing on school letterhead before their visit.

How to Get There:

From I-10, take exit 48 and head west on TX-118 (follow the signs). Travel about 10 miles until you come to a junction with another road. Turn left onto TX-118; you'll be on Davis Mountain Road for about 7 miles until you come to a second junction. Turn left again onto the historic site road and drove another mile to the park entrance.

GPS Coordinates:

30°35'57"N, 103°53'34"W

Nearest City or Town:

Aside from Fort Davis, the nearest town is Post, about 48 miles away.

Did You Know:

Fort Davis National Historic Site was built in 1854 as a US Army infantry outpost. It was under the command of Captain Randolph B. Marcy and used as a supply depot for US troops heading to New Mexico Territory. The fort served its purpose until 1861, when Confederate troops set off a bomb on its outside walls, causing them to collapse! So, soldiers rebuilt the walls but never used the fort again because they withdrew from this area after losing many battles against Mexican troops and Native Americans.

56. FORT WORTH BOTANIC GARDEN

Source: Kgredi76

Why You Should Visit:

Even if you're not a botanist, you'll enjoy exploring the trails filled with flowering plants, fragrant trees and shrubs, and beautiful flowers. There's also a fun maze, a gift shop, and a relaxing area filled with beautiful sculptures. Botany may not be your thing, but this beautiful garden is definitely worth visiting!

Location:

3220 Botanic Garden Blvd, Fort Worth, TX 76107, USA

Best Time to Visit:

It is most interesting during the spring when all the flowers bloom; the leaves are still green, and in the fall when the leaves change colors.

Pass/Permit/Fees:

For Children 6 to 15 years old: Free; $6; Adults: $12; Seniors(65+): $10

How to Get There:

From I-30, take exit 394, and drive west on University Drive for about a mile until you come to the intersection of University Drive and South University Drive. Head south on South University Drive for about 2 miles until you come to the intersection of South University Drive and Meadowbrook Road. Turn left onto Meadowbrook Road and drive north for about 1 mile until you arrive at the Meadowbrook Road intersection and Botanic Garden Boulevard. Turn right onto Botanic Garden Boulevard and drive west for about a quarter of a mile until you come to the intersection of Botanic Garden Boulevard with Aquilla Street. Turn right onto Aquilla Street, drive north for about 200 feet, then turn right into the entrance of Fort Worth Botanic Garden.

GPS Coordinates:

32° 44' 24.6444" N, 97° 21' 50.0472" W

Nearest City or Town:

Aside from Fort Worth, the nearest city is Grapevine, around 20 miles away!

Did You Know:

The botanic garden is a public garden containing a collection of living plants, not just their remains. Such gardens are educational institutions dedicated to the scientific study or cultivation of a large number of plants labeled with their botanical names. The Fort Worth Botanic Garden displays more than 3000 species with over 1 million individual plants covering 33 acres! This garden is also home to "Miss Lillian," a historic live oak tree that's been there for over 200 years!

58. FORT WORTH NATURE CENTER & REFUGE

Why You Should Visit:

Explore the beautiful scenic trails at this nature center and refuge. You can also see live animals, such as birds, reptiles, amphibians, wild pigs, and alligators. The refuge is also popular for bird watching, where you can spot white-tailed deer and other wildlife!

Location:

9601 Fossil Ridge Rd, Fort Worth, TX 76135, USA

Best Time to Visit:

The best time to go is in the spring, from March to May, when the cherry trees and spring flowers are in bloom. Also, at the beginning of July, a special event called "Wildflower Show" is held and attracts some visitors, mostly locals.

Pass/Permit/Fees:

For Children ages under 3: Free; For Children ages 3-12: $2; For Adults ages 13-64: $6; For Seniors ages 65+: $3; $1 Discount per person (with Military ID).

How to Get There:

From I-35, take exit 302 and head west on Exchange Avenue, and then continue west on Exchange Avenue for about 3 miles until you come to East Belknap Street. Turn right onto East Belknap Street and drive south for about 1/2 a mile until you come to the intersection of East Belknap Street and Fossil Ridge Road. Once there, turn left onto Fossil Ridge Road, then look for the Nature Center & Refuge sign on your left-hand side!

GPS Coordinates:

32.827317°N, 97.478913°W

Nearest City or Town:

Aside from Fort Worth, the nearest town is Benbrook, around 17 miles away.

Did You Know:

The Fort Worth Nature Center & Refuge was founded in 1969 by a nonprofit organization called the Nature Conservancy. The natural landscape, made up of gently rolling hills, wooded areas, and grassy fields, was preserved for future generations with the help of the City of Fort Worth.

58. FORT WORTH STOCKYARDS

Why You Should Visit:
Explore the past at this historic site, once one of the largest stockyards in the world. Today, you can see a variety of live animals, watch cowboy demonstrations, and listen to live music while taking a tour through the stockyards. Or you can soak up the atmosphere and explore on your own!

Location:
131 E Exchange Ave, Fort Worth, TX 76164, USA

Best Time to Visit:
April, May, September, October, and November are the best times to visit because of the mild weather.

Pass/Permit/Fees:
Free!

How to Get There:
From I-30, take exit 410, and drive east on Exchange Avenue for about half a mile until you come to the intersection of Exchange Avenue and E. Belknap Street. Turn left on E. Belknap Street and drive north for about a quarter mile until you reach the intersection of E. Belknap Street and East Exchange Avenue. Look for the entrance to Fort Worth Stockyards on your right-hand side!

GPS Coordinates:
32° 47' 18.8232" N, 97° 20' 46.4424" W

Nearest City or Town:
Aside from Fort Worth, the nearest city is Grapevine, around 20 miles away!

Did You Know:
The Fort Worth Stockyards is a large horned cattle exchange, built-in 1911 by George H. Murphy and operated by the Fort Worth Live Stock Exchange Company of Texas. The main purpose of the exchange was to bring in prime cattle from Texas and out-of-state rivers and streams for ship transport. During this time, Texas was still an independent country that was later annexed into the United States. The stockyards were a key piece to having Texas recognized by Mexico as an independent country back in 1836.

59. MARION SANSOM PARK

Why You Should Visit:

Take a walk and explore this urban park's trails that have a beautiful, scenic view of downtown Fort Worth and the Trinity River. There are also plenty of activities to do here, such as hiking, biking, running along the trails, picnicking in one of the many pavilions, or taking a leisurely stroll around Lake Como.

Location:

2501 Roberts Cut Off Rd, Fort Worth, TX 76114, USA

Best Time to Visit:

The best time to go is in the summer, from May to October, when the weather is nice, and there are lots of fun things to do at the park.

Pass/Permit/Fees:

Free!

How to Get There:

From I-30, take exit 410 and then head west on Exchange Avenue for about 3 miles until you come to the intersection with East Belknap Street. From there, turn right onto East Belknap Street and go about 2 miles till you reach the corner of East Belknap Street and Roberts Cut-Off Road. Turn left onto Roberts Cut-Off Road and drive for half a mile until you come to the parking lot on your left-hand side!

GPS Coordinates:

32.7955° N, 97.4132° W

Nearest City or Town:

Aside from Fort Worth, Saginaw is the closest city to this park, around 6 miles away.

Did You Know:

Marion Sansom Park was named after one of Fort Worth's prominent residents and business owners, Marion Sansom. She donated most of her land to the city for its use as a park. Mrs. Sansom's generosity went far beyond providing land for a park. She also provided funds for lake improvements and funding for the Martin Luther King Jr. Memorial Fountain in downtown Fort Worth (also known as "Little Berlin").

60. THE BALL-EDDLEMAN-MCFARLAND HOUSE

Source: Renelibrary

Why You Should Visit:

While most modern houses can be seen all over the city, there are only a few that have stood the test of time. From its construction in 1895 to today, this Victorian-style home has been preserved and refurbished. Now, you can tour this historic home and find out what life was like during the late 1800s!

Location:

1110 Penn St, Fort Worth, TX 76102, United States

Best Time to Visit:

March, April, and November are the best times to visit because of the mild weather.

Pass/Permit/Fees:

For the age of 12 and under: $10; For Adults: $20

How to Get There:

From I-30, take exit 410 and then head east on 4th St. for about 4 miles until you come to the intersection with Penn Street. Once there, turn right onto Penn Street and drive south for half a mile until you come to the intersection of Penn Street and Hickory Hill Drive.

GPS Coordinates:

32° 44.833′ N, 97° 20.56′ W

Nearest City or Town:

Aside from Fort Worth, the next closest town from this property is Arlington, around 10 miles away.

Did You Know:

The Ball-Eddleman-McFarland House was built in 1895 by John N. Ball, who was a successful businessman and rancher during the late 1800s. He was the owner of many ranches in Central Texas, and he owned the "Lost Creek Ranch," which supplied cattle to Fort Worth and other surrounding areas. The original owner sold it to his daughter, Ruth Eddleman, who lived there until her death at age 100. The house stayed in her family until it was purchased by a local insurance executive named Sam McFarland Jr.

61. LOG CABIN VILLAGE

Why You Should Visit:

Once you step foot on the grounds, you will find yourself inside a historical paradise that invites you to take an adventure in making memories. There are over 30 log cabins of varying sizes with many activities and places to explore. You can climb or jump off the large rock that is located at the center of Log Cabin Village. You can also enjoy a campfire, a few drinks at the outdoor bar, or go for a canoe trip in your very own canoe!

Location:

2100 Log Cabin Village Ln, Fort Worth, TX 76109, USA

Best Time to Visit:

The best time to visit is in February through October because of mild weather and no crowds (except on weekends)

Pass/Permit/Fees:

$7 per person (under 21, with valid ID). Children 5 and under are free.

How to Get There:

From I-30, take exit 410 and then head east on 4th St for about 4 miles until you come to the intersection with Carpenter Drive. Once there, turn left onto Carpenter Drive. Turn right onto Log Cabin Village Lane and drive for about 2 miles until you come to the parking lot on your right!

GPS Coordinates:

32.7202° N, 97.3616° W

Nearest City or Town:

Aside from Fort Worth, the next closest town from this property is Mansfield, which is located about 10 miles north of Log Cabin Village.

Did You Know:

The Log Cabin Village was originally built in 1982 as a miniature version of Fort Worth. It was expanded and renovated in 2002 to make it bigger and better than ever. There are over 30 log cabins that can be rented out for parties or events at the site.

62. ENCHANTED ROCK STATE NATURAL AREA

Source:Riofriotex

Why You Should Visit:

In the middle of West Texas is the Enchanted Rock State Natural Area. It is one of the most unique and amazing places to visit in Texas. The rocky formation makes it look like a magical playground, with more than 3,000 feet of natural cave formations (called "chimneys"). These breathtaking caves are lined with colorful tiered formations that are covered with a thick layer of soft soil. Entrances to the caves are located all over the top of this rock. A large staircase leads up to the top of the rock, and once you arrive, you will feel like you have entered a magical paradise.

Location:

16710 Ranch Rd 965, Fredericksburg, TX 78624, United States

Best Time to Visit:

April until October is the ideal time to go because it avoids very hot summer days and is before icy winter temperatures make this area untenable.

Pass/Permit/Fees:

A $3 entrance fee can be purchased at the park. Children 12 and under are free.

How to Get There:

From I-35, take exit 190A and head east on Ranch Rd 965 for almost 6 miles until you come to the park on your left-hand side! There is also an alternate route that you can take if you want to avoid Fredericksburg traffic. From I-10, take exit 161 (Dove Springs Road) and keep going through Dove Springs Road until it intersects with Ranch Rd 965 (about 5 miles) and then turn right onto Ranch Rd 965, which will take you right to the park.

GPS Coordinates:

30.4951° N, 98.8200° W

Nearest City or Town:

Aside from Fredericksburg, the closest towns to this park are Nolanville and Cleburne, both of which are located about 8 miles away.

Did You Know:

Some of the caves in this area date back 2 million years. The rock formation also resembles that of a snake. The name "Enchanted Rock" is derived from a local Native American tribe who used to refer to it as "Kulish-au-ha," - meaning "the snake that swallows its tail."

63. WILDSEED FARMS

Why You Should Visit:

Bring your camera and capture the ultimate in wildflower photographs at Wildseed Farms. A beautiful range of colors and textures can be found everywhere you turn. Plant life is abundant and is spread throughout the whole property. There are a variety of stops along the way that will allow you to take a picture of your favorite wildflower and nature lover!

Location:

100 Legacy Dr, 4. Pioneer Museum, TX 78624, USA

Best Time to Visit:

Spring and Fall (March through December) are the best weather months. Spring brings beautiful blooms and flowers, while Fall is a perfect time for pictures with fall foliage all around.

Pass/Permit/Fees:

$10 per vehicle, $5 per person on foot or bicycle (standing or riding). Children 12 and under are free.

How to Get There:

Take I-35, exit 190B, and head east on Ranch Road 965. Turn left onto Legacy Dr, which will take you right to the property on the left!

GPS Coordinates:

30° 13' 13.14" N, -98° 46' 3.41" W

Nearest City or Town:

Aside from FW, the next closest town to this property is Cleburne, which is located about 8 miles from the visitor center.

Did You Know:

Wildseed Farms has 200 acres of wildflowers in various stages of development. One of the most popular wildflowers is "Fire King," You may see many photographs of Wildseed Farms in the background. The Texas native "Gaillardia pulchella" is also a special favorite for many photographers.

64. PIONEER MUSEUM

Source: Liveon001 ©Travis K. Witt

Why You Should Visit:

The Pioneer Museum is an authentic collection of a Texas pioneer homestead dating back to 1882! It was restored in 2002 and, from then on, has been open to the public. The museum showcases the day-to-day life of West Texas pioneers through a variety of furnishing from the 1880s. Over 40 buildings on this land include a school, barn, blacksmith's shop, and more!

Location:

325 W Main St, Fredericksburg, TX 78624, United States

Best Time to Visit:

Even though it's open all year, the best times to visit are spring and fall because of the beautiful wildflowers and plants. This way, you can glimpse pioneer life during planting season or when they would be harvesting crops.

Pass/Permit/Fees:

There is a $5 fee for adults and $3 for children 12 and under. There are also other events during the year that you can attend for free!

How to Get There:

The museum is located about 6 blocks from I-35 in downtown Fredericksburg. There's plenty of parking space available along Main Street. If there are no spots in front of the building, parking can be found nearby on the street or in some of the lots adjacent to Main Street (please do not block any driveways). From I-35, take exit 190B, then head east on Ranch Road 965. Turn right onto Main St., and your first left is the museum!

GPS Coordinates:

30° 16' 42.2688" N, 98° 52' 38.9424" W

Nearest City or Town:

Aside from Fredericksburg, the closest town to this museum is Nolanville, which is only 7 miles away. From the property.

Did You Know:

The museum was built in 1882 by the Langston family. The building you see now was originally a barn that was later converted into living quarters. The Langstons first arrived on the property in 1855 and were among the first settlers of Gillespie County.

65. FORT MARTIN SCOTT

Why You Should Visit:

The United States Army built Fort Martin Scott in 1848. It was the first fort built between San Antonio and Mexico. This landmark is often used as a backdrop in movies, such as over 20 different movies since the 1920s. Visit this historical fort to see what one of the first battles was like between Texas Rangers and Mexican Army in 1848.

Location:

1606 E Main St, Fredericksburg, TX 78624, United States

Best Time to Visit:

Summer is a great time to visit the fort because of the beautiful wildflowers and foliage. If you have not been here before, this will be a great time to explore the fort because it is very open and light!

Pass/Permit/Fees:

There are no fees to visit the fort, but parking can sometimes be limited.

How to Get There:

The fort is located about 3 blocks east of I-35, and Main St. Turn right onto E Main St and head to the second driveway on the right just after you pass the visitor center. Follow the road to the fort.

GPS Coordinates:

30° 13' 16.284" N, 98° 45' 52.344" W

Nearest City or Town:

Aside from Fredericksburg, the closest town to this fort is Johnson City, which is about 14 miles east of the fort.

Did You Know:

Named after Martin Collier Scott, who was a volunteer during the Mexican American War. He died in 1851 at the Battle of Monterrey, where he fought for Mexico.

66. WILLOW CITY LOOP

Why You Should Visit:

This trail is located on the Willow City Loop Ranch. It consists of a 3.7-mile hard surface path that allows you to get a car-free experience of the Texas countryside as you walk or ride your bike through the working cattle ranch, the wide-open fields, and the natural springs. In addition, you will have opportunities to see wildlife and even a few bison.

Location:

Willow City Loop, Willow City, TX 78624, United States

Best Time to Visit:

The best times to see wildflowers and animals are in the spring and fall.

Pass/Permit/Fees:

There is a $5 vehicle fee and a $5 park entrance fee.

How to Get There:

Take I-35 North to Exit #190. Go east on W Main Street/TX-30 and follow it for 2 miles. Turn left onto FM 1874 for about 1 mile, then turn left onto a gravel road that leads to the property entrance.

GPS Coordinates:

30° 24' 1.79" N, -98° 42' 2.99" W

Nearest City or Town:

The nearest city to this location is Junction, about 15 miles away.

Did You Know:

Willow City Loop is a working cattle ranch and has been in operation since the mid-1800s. The same family still runs it!

67. 1892 BISHOP'S PALACE

Why You Should Visit:

Here is where you should go to get away from the crowds and relax. The Bishop's Palace is a beautiful Victorian home that the Galveston Diocese used to provide assistance to orphans. Today, it is open for public tours that walk you through the history of the building and show you around each room. If you want to learn about the past of Texas, this is a great place to go.

Location:

1402 Broadway Avenue J, Galveston, TX 77550, USA

Best Time to Visit:

The best times to visit are from November through February. The weather is cooler and less humid than the other months in Galveston, and the best times to see the house in its full glory are during these months.

Pass/Permit/Fees:

For ages 5 and under: Free; For ages 6-18: $9; Adult: $15.

How to Get There:

Take I-45 south to the Harborside Drive exit. Go west on Harborside Drive to Broadway Avenue, turn left, and continue to 14th Street. Turn right and proceed to the 3rd gate across from the Galveston Island Convention Center.

GPS Coordinates:

29°18'17" N, 94°46'55" W

Nearest City or Town:

Aside from Galveston, the closest town to this property is La Marque, which is about 10 miles away.

Did You Know:

The building is named after Bishop Emilio G. García, who served as the bishop of Galveston from 1881-1897 and then as the bishop of San Antonio from 1897-1902.

68. THE SEAWALL

Why You Should Visit:

The Seawall is a drive along Galveston Bay! It is a beautiful drive that will give you endless views of the beautiful Gulf of Mexico while being able to smell the salty sea air. The scenery is great, and the breeze is wonderful. The photo opportunities are endless. If you are looking for a great, scenic drive, this is the place for you!

Location:

Galveston, TX 77550, United States

Best Time to Visit:

The months of June through September are the best time to view the Seawall due to the clear, sunny skies and warm weather.

Pass/Permit/Fees:

There are no fees to visit the Seawall.

How to Get There:

Take I-45 South to Galveston Island, then follow Highway 87 south to 61st Street. Drive East on 61st Street to The Strand and the Seawall.

GPS Coordinates:

29° 18' 5.40" N, -94° 46' 16.79" W

Nearest City or Town:

Aside from Galveston, the closest town to this drive is Baytown, which is about 20 miles north of the seawall.

Did You Know:

The seawall originally began as a wagon road in 1854, with its purpose being to transport goods along the beach. That year, it was damaged by a hurricane and changed into a sand dune that was later created into a barrier from the Gulf. The entire seawall project took place between 1902 and 1905.

69. MOODY MANSION

Why You Should Visit:

If you want to see a once-in-a-lifetime piece of Texas history, then the Moody Mansion is for you! This mansion is a huge Victorian home that was once the residence of Texas Governor and Galveston County District Attorney James Stephen Hogg and his wife, Ima. The house was built in 1892 by George C. Toomer and had over 12,000 square feet of living area. You will be able to see the original wallpaper and woodwork throughout the house!

Location:

2618 Broadway Avenue J, Galveston, TX 77550, USA

Best Time to Visit:

The months of June through September are the best times to view the mansion. During these months, the sun is very low in the sky and casts ghostly shadows across its front porch, making it look even eerier than it already is. This mansion is perfect for hot summer days!

Pass/Permit/Fees:

Guided All-Access Tours: $35/Person

How to Get There:

Take I-45 south to the Harborside Drive exit. Go west on Harborside Drive to Broadway Avenue, turn left, and continue to 14th Street. Turn right and proceed to the 3rd gate across from the Galveston Island Convention Center.

GPS Coordinates:

29.2995° N, 94.7963° W

Nearest City or Town:

Aside from Galveston, the closest town to this location is La Marque, which is about 10 miles away.

Did You Know:

The Moody Mansion was built in 1892 by George C. Toomer and contained 12,000 square feet of living area. It is one of the only buildings left in Galveston that survived the hurricane of 1900!

70. GALVESTON'S 61ST STREET FISHING PIER

Source: Jim Evans

Why You Should Visit:
The colorful fishing pier at 61st Street is a great place for fishing! The pier is equipped with lights and fishing platforms so you can get the best view of the sunset and catch the day's dinner. It is also a great place to watch ships as they pass by or enjoy the cool breeze as you walk along the pier.

Location:
6101 Seawall Blvd, Galveston, TX 77551, USA

Best Time to Visit:
The best times to visit are during the months of June through September. The weather is cooler and less humid than the other months of the year and provides a great time to see the ocean from the pier.

Pass/Permit/Fees:
The admission fee varies from $6.00 - $30.50 depending

How to Get There:
Take I-45 south to Galveston, then follow Highway 87 north to 61st Street. Turn right onto 61st Street and proceed three blocks north until you reach the end of the street at the Seawall.

GPS Coordinates:
29°21'31" N, 94°49'7" W

Nearest City or Town:
The closest town to the pier in Galveston, which is about 20 minutes away by car. The next closest town is League City, which is about 20 miles north of the pier.

Did You Know:
The pier was first built in 1927 and rebuilt again in 1948 after a devastating hurricane hit the area. Originally built by developers Milford Howard and Ralph Fults, it was donated to Galveston in 1986. In 2005, Hurricane Rita destroyed most fishing piers along the Texas coast, but this pier survived because it was at sea level and not as high up as many other piers. During Hurricane Ike, many fishermen returned to Moody Beach State Park for refuge during Hurricane Ike's arrival.

71. CENTRAL TEXAS OLIVE RANCH

Why You Should Visit:

The farm is home to hundreds of olive trees, which are hand-picked and then sold at different times throughout the year. If you're looking for a unique traveling experience, this is it! It is also a great place to photograph because of its scenery and the rustic buildings that surround the trees.

Location:

564 County Road 715, Georgetown, TX 78627 USA

Best Time to Visit:

The farm is open all year round but is best viewed during the months of April through November. This is when you will be able to see the olives being harvested and sold for around $7.00 - $9.00 per pound!

Pass/Permit/Fees:

There is no admission fee to view the ranch, but you must pay for the olives that you purchase.

How to Get There:

Take Highway 69 south from Georgetown and exit at County Road 715 West. Take County Road 715 west until it reaches the farm's entrance and parking lot. (If you are coming from I-35, take Exit 42 - Georgetown-Cameron to State Highway 69 West toward Lucas and turn right onto FM 1401W) Following FM 1401W until you reach CR 715 West/County Road 415, continue west. Turn south onto CR 715 (about 3/4 mile past the bridge) and look for signs.

GPS Coordinates:

30° 37' 59.7432" N and 97° 40' 40.7424" W

Nearest City or Town:

Aside from the town of Georgetown, the farm is about 4 miles away from the town of Liberty Hill. The closest city is Austin, which is about 65 miles west.

Did You Know:

This farm is one of many olive farms in Texas that produces a variety of olives! Besides producing olives, this family-owned business also presents children with various educational opportunities related to agriculture and life on a ranch - including daily science lessons and field trips! The family has even started "olive school," an award-winning program where children can learn everything they need to know about growing olives!

72. HISTORIC WILLIAMSON COUNTY COURTHOUSE

Source: Larry D. Moore

Why You Should Visit:

This courthouse was constructed from 1852 to 1859 after the county separated from Angelina County. This historic building is one of Texas's best examples of Greek Revival architecture! It is located in the Williamson County Courthouse Historic District, making it one of only three courthouses in Texas listed on the National Register of Historic Places.

The courthouse is often used for weddings and photo shoots because it has many great features, including a historic rotunda and a tower.

Location:

710 S Main St, Georgetown, TX 78626, USA

Best Time to Visit:

The best times to visit are from April through November when the courthouse is open for tours. You can also visit during the spring and fall for different concerts, which are held at the Courthouse Square.

Pass/Permit/Fees:

There is no admission fee to view the building, but the parking will cost you approximately $7.00 - $9.00 per day.

GPS Coordinates:

30° 38' 13.3152" N, 97° 40' 39.0756" W

Nearest City or Town:

After visiting the courthouse, you are welcome to stop at the old town of Georgetown to see some of the other historical buildings. It is about 3 miles from the courthouse and was established in 1848. There are plenty of shops and restaurants to visit, so you will have a fun time with your family walking around!

Did You Know:

Williamson County has a lot of historic sites that show how the county went from being on the frontier to be one of the most important agricultural counties in Texas. Dallas may be a larger city now, but this county holds much more history than many people realize.

73. INNER SPACE CAVERN

Why You Should Visit:

This cave is one of the only known caves in Texas that has a natural entrance! It is estimated to be around 300 million years old, which means it was created during the Pennsylvanian period. It has over 2 miles of passages and is filled with stalagmites, stalactites, soda straws, and rimstones. If you are an adventurer, you will love exploring the dark and mysterious cave!

Location:

7408 Main St, San Antonio, TX 78217 USA

Best Time to Visit:

This cavern is best visited during the months of March through October. The cave is not open during the summer because of the high temperatures.

Pass/Permit/Fees:

$12.95 for children; and $20.95 for adult admission.

GPS Coordinates:

30°36'28" N, 97°41'16" W

Nearest City or Town:

San Antonio is about 10 miles south of the cave.

Did You Know:

The Inner Space Cavern is home to several endangered species of animals, including a blind salamander called an Olm, which is found only in the cave. The cavern is also home to cave crickets and cave shrimp!

74. GRANBURY CITY BEACH PARK

Source: Michael Barera

Why You Should Visit:
This beach is a relatively calm, shallow bay that is great for swimming and fun in the sun. The surf here is not rough, and the water is warm, clear, and clean. There are many other recreational opportunities in this area as well, including volleyball courts, picnic tables, and a playground. You can even see the Santa Fe railroad as it goes by.

Location:
505 E Pearl St, Granbury, TX 76048, United States

Best Time to Visit:
The months of June through September are the best time to view this beach due to the warm, clear weather and low surf. During the day, you will find yourself alone on this beach for hours, exploring the nature around you. As for nighttime fun, many restaurants and bars around Granbury provide entertainment during this time of day.

Pass/Permit/Fees:
The parking fee is $3.00/day, and the admission fee is $1.00/day

How to Get There:
Take I-35 north to exit 542 for TX-114/FM1174 west toward Granbury. Turn right onto TX-114 (0.8 miles), then left onto FM-2498 (2 miles). Go 2 miles, cross the bridge over Lake Granbury, turn left at the next light, then turn right at the second light to reach the parking lot on your left.

GPS Coordinates:
32° 26' 31.4988" N, 97° 47' 39.1092" W

Nearest City or Town:
This site is located in Granbury, which is about 20 minutes southwest of Fort Worth.

Did You Know:

Lake Granbury has been the site of several popular movies and commercials since it was built in 1967, including Peter Bogdanovich's "The Last Picture Show" (1971) and the pilot episode for the TV show Walker Texas Ranger (1993). It was also featured in commercials for Budweiser beer, the Nissan Altima automobile model, and a 2005 ad for Drakkar cologne. Most recently, it was used as a filming location for "Texas Chainsaw 3D" (2013)

75. BUFFALO SOLDIERS NATIONAL MUSEUM

Why You Should Visit:

If you enjoy history or have family members who have served in the military, this museum may interest you! This museum was established to commemorate the African-American soldiers who fought during several wars, including The American Civil War, Spanish–American War, the Philippine Insurrection, and World War I. Many exhibits are dedicated to educating visitors about the experience of African-Americans in the United States Military. This museum is one of the few places in the country where you can view items from both World War II and Vietnam, which many people find fascinating.

Location:

3816 Caroline St, Houston, TX 77004, USA

Best Time to Visit:

The months of June through October are the best times to visit this museum due to low humidity and weather conditions. There is always something happening at Buffalo Soldiers National Museum!

Pass/Permit/Fees:

The admission fee is $15.00/adult and $12.00/senior, with children under 12 free.

How to Get There:

Take I-45 north to Highway 45 West, then continue west on Highway 45 until you reach 37th Street (approximately 20 miles). Take a right onto 37th Street and proceed one block north until you reach Caroline Street. On the corner of Caroline and Capitol Streets is where the museum.

GPS Coordinates:

29° 44' 9.5064" N, 95° 22' 41.268" W

Nearest City or Town:

Aside from Houston, the closest city is Pasadena, which is approximately 15 miles north of this museum.

Did You Know:

Buffalo Soldiers National Museum has a special collection that includes original Civil War uniforms and other artifacts. The museum also hosts many special events, including the annual National African American History Month Celebration.

76. SPACE CENTER HOUSTON

Source: Michael Barera

Why You Should Visit:

This is the perfect place for anyone who loves history and space exploration. This museum provides a detailed look at the space industry and its role in society, past and present. You can see all the programs that NASA has had over time, space missions launched, and much more!

Location:

1601 E NASA Pkwy, Houston, TX 77058, USA

Best Time to Visit:

The best time to visit this space center is during the summer when it is not very hot. The crowds are smaller at this time of year, and you can get a close-up look at some of the cool artifacts they have on display.

Pass/Permit/Fees:

Admission to this museum is $15.00 for adults and $13.00 for seniors; children under 12 are free!

How to Get There:

Take Highway 290 north to Highway 610, then continue north on 610 until it merges with I-45 North/US 75 North/US 290. From there, take I-45 North to NASA Road 1, turn left on NASA Road 1 (approximately 4 miles), and continue straight until it intersects with NASA Parkway. Turn left and follow NASA Parkway until you reach the space center.

GPS Coordinates:

29° 33' 6.77" N, -95° 05' 54.03" W

Nearest City or Town:

Aside from Houston, the next city from this location is The Woodlands, which is approximately 15 miles northeast of this museum.

Did You Know:

Over 1.4 million people visit the Space Center Houston every year, making it one of the most popular museums in Texas. The museum is also known for its special exhibits, which have included moon rock displays and a replica of the ISS.

77. SAM HOUSTON PARK

Why You Should Visit:

Sam Houston Park is within walking distance from the Texas Capitol, making it the perfect place to go for a walk after you visit the state capitol. The park is home to many fun things you can do and see, including an aviary, botanical gardens, a zoo, and monuments. This park also has several historical sites that any history buff would love to see.

Location:

1000 Bagby St, Houston, TX 77002, United States

Best Time to Visit:

There is never a bad time to come and enjoy Sam Houston Park's beauty. You can visit this park year-round and enjoy a variety of things, such as nature, wildlife, and more!

Pass/Permit/Fees:

There is no admission fee for this park, but donations are accepted. There is also no permit required.

How to Get There:

Take I-45 south to Highway 288, exit Highway 288, heading west towards downtown Houston (approximately 1 mile). Take Bagby Street, which will be on your left (approximately 1 mile). Turn right onto Capitol Street and go one block until you reach Sam Houston Park on your left.

GPS Coordinates:

29.7601° N, 95.3716° W

Nearest City or Town:

Aside from Houston, the closest city is The Woodlands, which is approximately 10 miles northeast of Sam Houston Park.

Did You Know:

Rated as one of the top ten parks in Texas, Sam Houston Park was founded in 1854 by Thomas G. McFarland and Robert E. Lee, who donated part of their own land to build the park.

78. BATTLESHIP TEXAS

Why You Should Visit:

With the state capitol right next door and the Battleship Texas Museum right down the street, you can see the history of Texas in one place. You can learn about over seven decades of military service for US Navy personnel, including World War II and The Cuban Missile Crisis. If you're an aviation buff, you can see the carrier, USS Lexington.

Location:

One Riverway Suite 2200, Houston, TX 77056, United States

Best Time to Visit:

The best time to visit this museum is during the summer and fall when it is not very hot outside. You can get nice, cool weather for free at Battleship Texas!

Pass/Permit/Fees:

Entry to this museum is $10.00 for adults and $7.00 for children, with children under 6 free.

How to Get There:

Take Highway 288 south to Highway 3 (approximately 6 miles). Take Highway 3 North towards downtown Houston (approximately 5 miles). Take Interstate 45 North until it merges with Highway 288 West (approximately 2 miles). Exit onto West Dallas Street, turn right on McKinney Street and continue forward onto the main entrance of Battleship Texas.

GPS Coordinates:

29.7634° N, 95.4613° W

Nearest City or Town:

Aside from Houston, the nearest city is Galveston, which is approximately 45 miles north of this museum.

Did You Know:

Battleship Texas was the second ship of its class, built during World War II to protect the US from invasions from Japan. The ship was placed in service on 1 March 1944.

79. PEDERNALES FALLS STATE PARK

Why You Should Visit:

This park is a great place for nature lovers. Pedernales Falls is a waterfall that is over 200 feet high and drops down over a cliff that you can walk to the bottom of. Explore the park's many hiking trails, picnic areas, and more.

Location:

2585 Park Rd 6026, Johnson City, TX 78636, United States

Best Time to Visit:

The best time to visit this park is during the spring and fall months when the weather is not so hot. During this time, the falls are more likely to be flowing, and the crowds are much smaller.

Pass/Permit/Fees:

There is an entrance fee of $6.00 for adults and $3.00 for children under 12 years old, with children under 6 free. There is no permit required for this park that we could find!

How to Get There:

Take Highway 290 west towards Johnson City (approximately 26 miles). Turn left onto Park Road 6026, leading into Pedernales Falls State Park (approximately .7 miles)

GPS Coordinates:

30.3081° N, 98.2577° W

Nearest City or Town:

Aside from Johnson City, the nearest town is San Marcos, which is approximately 20 miles southeast of Pedernales Falls State Park.

Did You Know:

This park is a great place to go for a summer camping trip! You can hike through the park, see the falls, and enjoy nature at its finest.

80. CADDO LAKE STATE PARK

Source: Jay Carriker

Why You Should Visit:

If your adventuring spirit is strong enough, you can kayak or canoe right up to the falls at Caddo Lake State Park. This lake is known for its fishing and fishing tournaments, thus giving this park a sporty feel rather than just a natural one.

Location:

245 Park Rd 2, Karnack, TX 75661, United States

Best Time to Visit:

The best time to visit this park is from March through October. This is when the weather is slightly cooler, and you aren't as likely to need a jacket or raincoat. During this time, the lake will be warmer and less crowded than during the other seasons.

Pass/Permit/Fees:

There is an entrance fee of $5.00 for adults (ages 12 and older) and $2.00 for children ages 6-11 years old, with children under 6 free.

How to Get There:

Take Highway 80 east towards Rusk (approximately 6 miles). Exit onto Park Road 5400, leading into Caddo Lake State Park (approximately 11 miles).

GPS Coordinates:

32.68712° N, -94.18018° W

Nearest City or Town:

Aside from being just a few minutes away from the city of Marshall, the nearest city is Nacogdoches, which is approximately 50 miles southwest of Caddo Lake State Park.

Did You Know:

Caddo Lake State Park is home to over 200 species of wildlife, wildflowers, and a variety of trees. The lake is also home to many fish and other animals, including alligators!

81. KEMAH BOARDWALK

Why You Should Visit:

This boardwalk is one of the oldest in Texas and is still highly frequented by tourists and locals alike. Many shows, shops, and restaurants are located along the 1.8-mile boardwalk. Watch some outdoor movies on the beach or visit one of the many local events!

Location:

215 Kipp Ave, Kemah, TX 77565, United States

Best Time to Visit:

The months of July through October are the best time to visit the Kemah Boardwalk because it is not so hot and the crowds are less. During this time, you can enjoy all of these things without rushing.

Pass/Permit/Fees:

Entry to this boardwalk is free for anyone.

How to Get There:

Take Highway 35 south towards Galveston (approximately 22 miles). Turn right onto Interstate 45 North, leading into Kemah. Turn right on Kipp Avenue, leading into the Kemah Boardwalk (approximately 1.8 miles).

GPS Coordinates:

29.5473° N, 95.0202° W

Nearest City or Town:

Aside from Kemah, the nearest town is Bay City, which is approximately 26 miles east of this boardwalk in Galveston County.

Did You Know:

Over 130 shops, restaurants, and attractions are located along the Kemah Boardwalk, making it a great place to take an afternoon stroll and walk off some of that boardwalk burger you ate!

82. ROY E. LARSEN SANDYLAND SANCTUARY

Source: Palustris.ETX

Why You Should Visit:

From bird watching to hiking, this sanctuary has a lot to offer any adventurer. It is also home to numerous plant species, including one of Texas's last longleaf pine trees. There are many different trails to take through the sanctuary and various other things to do. If you appreciate nature and animals, this is the place for you.

Location:

4208 TX-327, Kountze, TX 77625, USA

Best Time to Visit:

March through November is the best time to visit this sanctuary. There are fewer bugs and fewer people during this time frame. During these months, you will have your own personal sanctuary to enjoy!

Pass/Permit/Fees:

There is an entrance fee of $5.00 per person.

How to Get There:

Take Highway 87 west towards Beaumont (approximately 24 miles). Continue on Highway 87 until it turns into Highway 327. Follow this for a little less than ten miles until you reach the entrance of the sanctuary on the right-hand side (approximately 6 miles).

GPS Coordinates:

30.3615978°N, -94.2476871°W

Nearest City or Town:

Aside from Beaumont, the nearest town is Orange, which is approximately 25 miles northeast of Kountze.

Did You Know:

This sanctuary is home to over 100 different types of birds, including the endangered golden-cheeked warbler.

83. GORMAN FALLS

Why You Should Visit:

If you're looking for a place to cool off, look at Gorman Falls. Located near the bayou in a 9-acre park, this spot is popular for swimming and hiking. This park also boasts much wildlife, which includes alligators, deer, and pheasants.

Location:

Gorman Falls Trail, Lometa, TX 76853, United States

Best Time to Visit:

The best months to visit this spot are January, February, and March because the temperatures are cooler, and you don't have to worry about mosquitoes.

Pass/Permit/Fees:

Admission is free.

How to Get There:

From I-35, take exit 830 for TX-83 towards TX-27/TX-141. Take a right onto TX-83 South towards Lometa (approximately 2 miles). Continue forward onto TX-323 Spur North/TX-27 (approximately 1 mile). Take a slight left to stay on TX-323 Spur North/TX -27, which will be on your right (approximately 0.3 miles). Continue forward onto FM 1697 North/FM 1802 West until you reach the park entrance.

GPS Coordinates:

31° 3' 37.0944" N, 98° 29' 3.426" W

Nearest City or Town:

Aside from Lometa, the nearest city is Houston, which is approximately 3 miles northwest of this park.

Did You Know:

The Gorman Falls area was initially settled by settlers in 1836, and the settlement was known as Gorman's Bluff. The name of the park changed twice before becoming Gorman Falls, which is named after George B. Gorman, who owned a store and gristmill in what is now Lometa.

84. MARFA LIGHTS VIEWING AREA

Why You Should Visit:

Marfa Lights Viewing Area is the perfect spot to watch one of Texas's most famous unexplained phenomena. There have been sightings dating back thousands of years, and people today still cannot figure out what makes them appear. The lights are thought to be caused by car headlights or something similar, but scientists have never been able to explain the lights. If you're interested in seeing these lights for yourself, this is the place to be!

Location:

US-90, Marfa, TX 79843, USA

Best Time to Visit:

The best months that will guarantee you a viewing opportunity are October, November, and December, during late evening hours when the sky is dark.

Pass/Permit/Fees:

There is no entry fee to this viewing area.

How to Get There:

From the intersection of I-10 and US-90 in Midland, take US-90 towards El Paso, TX (approximately 15 miles). Take a slight left onto TX-17/TX-54, which will be on your right (approximately 0.4 miles). Continue forward onto FM 802 North/FM 174 West until you reach the viewing area.

GPS Coordinates:

30.2751° N, 103.8828° W

Nearest City or Town:

Aside from Marfa, the nearest town is Alpine, which is approximately 10 miles south of this viewing area.

Did You Know:

The earliest recorded sighting of the Marfa Lights was in 1783 by a Spanish missionary traveling through the region. Real-time cameras are now set up to film the lights at night so that scientists can study them.

85. MATAGORDA BAY NATURE PARK

Source: Larry D. Moore

Why You Should Visit:

If you are a nature lover and want to see the best of the best, take a trip south of Houston to Matagorda Bay Nature Park. The park spans over 4,300 acres of land and features around 30 miles of trails so that you can get up close with all of Texas' beautiful animals. From black bears to coyotes, this park is a great place for wildlife enthusiasts.

Location:

6430 FM Rd 2031, Matagorda, TX 77457, USA

Best Time to Visit:

Summer months, from March to August, are the best time to visit.

Pass/Permit/Fees:

The park is free to visit, with no pass required.

How to Get There:

Take US Highway 77 south towards Galveston. After you pass Seawall Boulevard, take a left onto FM 2031. Follow FM 2031 for 5 miles until it merges with Highway 35 (approximately 12 miles). Take Highway 35 towards Rockport, and turn right on State Park Road (approximately 9 miles). At the end of State Park Road, turn left onto Primrose Lane (it will be on your left) and continue forward until you reach the park entrance.

GPS Coordinates:

29.9992° N, 95.1805° W

Nearest City or Town:

Aside from Matagorda, the nearest city to this park is Rockport, which is approximately 20 miles south of this spot.

Did You Know:

The land that is now Matagorda Bay Nature Park was once part of a plantation from 1844 to 1910. The plantation is named after the bay on the opposite side of the peninsula from where the park is today.

86. GRUENE HISTORIC DISTRICT

Why You Should Visit:
If you love country music and want to see part of Texas' history, visit the Gruene Historic District, which is famous for its Twin Gruene Covered Bridges and the Gruene Hall of Texas Folklore Museum. This historic district is known for its yearly music festival, The Texas Motordome, which is one of the biggest in Texas. One of the oldest structures in this area is the Gruene Pioneer Museum, which was built in 1891 and is currently a museum.

Location:
1601 Hunter Rd New Braunfels, TX 78130

Best Time to Visit:
This would be a great place to visit during the spring and fall months. During the summer, it can get too hot and humid for comfort.

Pass/Permit/Fees:
There is no fee or permit required when you come to this museum. However, the Gruene Hall of Texas Folklore Museum does cost $4.00 for adults and $2.00 for children.

How to Get There:
From I-35, you can take Highway 90 past New Braunfels and take FM 471 South toward Fredericksburg. After you pass Fredericksburg, take a left on US 87. This will be approximately 23 miles from I-35/I-37 (approximately an hour's drive in total) once you take Highway 87. Follow Highway 87 until it merges with Highway 27. Turn left onto Woodlawn Road and continue forward onto Gruene Road.

GPS Coordinates:
29° 44' 21.048" N, 98° 6' 17.5716" W

Nearest City or Town:
Aside from New Braunfels, the nearest city is San Antonio, which is approximately a 35-minute drive to the south.

Did You Know:
Americans for the Arts voted the Gruene Historic District as the second "Best Place to Live in Texas" in 2009.

87. STONEHENGE REPLICA

Why You Should Visit:

If you love history and want to see a replica of the mysterious Stonehenge in England, visit the Odessa Stonehenge. This is much smaller than the original, but it still has that same mystique that surrounds the original. It is located right next to the park where you can picnic with friends and family (remember your dog!).

Location:

Preston Smith Rd, Odessa, TX 79762, USA

Best Time to Visit:

The months of October, November, and April are the best months to visit this spot, as the weather is typically nice during these months.

Pass/Permit/Fees:

The park entrance fee is $3.00 for adults and $1.00 for children. The United States Park Service recommends no visits by children under the age of 13 for safety reasons, as there is a possibility that some children may be injured if they play too close to the location.

How to Get There:

Take Highway 158 West to Preston Smith Road to Pecan Park Road (approximately 24 miles). This is approximately 2.8 miles south of mile marker 15 on Highway 385. There are signs directing you once you are close to the actual park.

GPS Coordinates:

31.8919° N, 102.3262° W

Nearest City or Town:

Aside from Odessa, the closest city is Midland, which is approximately 20 miles southwest of this site.

Did You Know:

This replica of Stonehenge was built by members of a local Masonic lodge, with the approval of the other lodges. When you visit this unique location, you can also see that there is a great view of the Texas plains from this site.

88. LAKE BOB SANDLIN STATE PARK

Source: OmgWhizBoyOmg

Why You Should Visit:

Enjoy a relaxing day of fishing, swimming, and other fun activities at this beautiful state park. Lake Bob Sandlin is bordered by forest and provides visitors with many opportunities to spot wildlife, fish, boat, and camp in the great outdoors. It is also located near other great Texas attractions, so it is a perfect place to take a day trip when you are looking for something new to explore!

Location:

341 State, Park Rd 2117, Pittsburg, TX 75686, United States

Best Time to Visit:

The month of May is the best time to visit this state park, as the weather is typically ideal for outdoor activities.

Pass/Permit/Fees:

This state park is absolutely free to enter!

How to Get There:

Take Highway 87 North toward Mineral Wells and exit at Park Road 2117 East. Turn right onto Park Road 2117 East, then take a left onto State Street, which will be on your left. The entrance to the park will be on your right after you have turned onto State Street.

GPS Coordinates:

30.1784° N, 97.0082° W

Nearest City or Town:

Aside from Pittsburg, the closest city is Mineral Wells, which is approximately 45 miles southwest of this park location.

Did You Know:

This park was named Texas' first park in 1972 by the Texas Parks and Wildlife Department. The lakes in the area were also named for Bob Sandlin, who lived nearby.

89. PORT ARANSAS FISHERMANS WHARF

Why You Should Visit:

This beautiful waterfront of Port Aransas is where you'll find the Port Aransas Fisherman's Wharf, a perfect place for families to gather. The Fisherman's Wharf features many fun activities for visitors, including fishing, swimming, sunbathing, and more! It also has many food stands and shops where you can get snacks and souvenirs. This is a great place to go if you want to spend a day relaxing on the coast.

Location:

900 Tarpon St, Port Aransas, TX 78373, USA

Best Time to Visit:

The summer is the best time to go to Port Aransas because the weather isn't too hot or cold. It can get very cold in the winter months, and there is little to do but walk along the main road.

Pass/Permit/Fees:

There is no entrance fee for this great place! There may be a few fees for activities, such as fishing and diving.

How to Get There:

Take Highway 361 North toward Port Aransas. Turn left onto 31st Street, then turn right onto Tarpon Street, which will be on your right. This will lead you straight to the Fisherman's Wharf.

GPS Coordinates:

27° 50' 2.0976" N and 97° 3' 39.9456" W

Nearest City or Town:

Aside from Port Aransas, the closest town is Corpus Christi, which is approximately 10 miles northwest of this location.

Did You Know:

The city purchased the Port Aransas Fisherman's Wharf in May 1967 and rebuilt it to be a fisherman's wharf in 1969. It has been paved since then and has hosted many events over the years.

90. HALFMOON REEF LIGHTHOUSE

Source: Charles Henry

Why You Should Visit:

Have you ever seen a lighthouse out in the ocean before? If not, there's one for you to see at Halfmoon Reef Lighthouse! Here you can see a lighthouse that has been in a number of films and TV shows. This lighthouse also has a settlement built directly behind it, where you can see the buildings and steps that were built to protect the lighthouse. You should definitely take some time to see this lighthouse because it's very interesting!

Location:

2300 TX-35, Port Lavaca, TX 77979, United States

Best Time to Visit:

The best time to visit this lighthouse is during the summer months because that's when visitors are able to see the most beautiful water and weather conditions. In the winter months, it can get very cold here.

Pass/Permit/Fees:

None

How to Get There:

Take Highway 35 towards Port Lavaca, TX. Turn right onto Bay Street (TX-35) and continue south until you reach 23rd Street. Take a left onto 23rd Street and then turn right onto South Beach Road, which will lead you straight to the lighthouse on your left!

GPS Coordinates:

28°38'12.8" N, 96°37'2.2" W

Nearest City or Town:

Aside from Port Lavaca, the nearest city is Corpus Christi, which is about 70 miles away from this lighthouse.

Did You Know:

Halfmoon Reef Lighthouse has a history with the Civil War as Colonel A. S. Brown supported Texas' independence from Mexico. When the War of Northern Aggression began, he traveled to Mexico, where he volunteered in an effort to gain independence for his area of Texas. He was eventually made a Colonel and was given authority over the local area by President Lincoln and then-Governor Sam Houston during the war.

91. ISLAND VIEW PARK

Why You Should Visit:

Island View Park is a wonderful place to visit because of its beautiful scenery! In fact, this park is the only place in Texas where you can have a picnic and see both the Gulf of Mexico and the Intracoastal Waterway Canal, which are both right here in the park.

Location:

87426 Preston Bend Rd, Pottsboro, TX 75076, United States

Pass/Permit/Fees:

The pass fee is $15.00 for adults from July 1 to September 30; $10 for adults from October 1 to June 30; $7 for seniors any time of year; and children under 6 are free.

Best Time to Visit:

The best time to go to this park is in the summer, when it's the hottest. Visitors can go to the park in the fall and see leaves from a distance.

How to Get There:

Take Highway 281 South toward Pottsboro. After you go about one mile, turn right onto Reliance Road (TX-275). Stay on this road for approximately 3 miles until it ends at Preston Bend Road. Turn right onto Preston Bend Road and continue until you see Island View Park on your right!

GPS Coordinates:

27°13'36.85" N and 96°16'9.47" W

Nearest City or Town:

Aside from Pottsboro, the closest city is Weatherford, which is approximately 45 miles southwest of this park location.

Did You Know:

This park was created by the Pottsboro Community Development Association and was officially opened in June of 1981. In 1982, the park began hosting the "Potts County Festival," a summertime event that features food, crafts, and live entertainment.

92. MCNAY ART MUSEUM

Source: Zereshk

Why You Should Visit:

If you're a fan of art, the McNay Art Museum is definitely worth visiting! They have a great collection of art, and the museum itself is a piece of art. Marion Koogler McNay, an American painter and art teacher, gave this 24-room mansion in the Spanish colonial revival style and a large collection of her own art. The museum is mostly about European and American art from the 19th and 20th centuries. It has some great works by Paul Cezanne, Pablo Picasso, Paul Gauguin, Henri Matisse, Georgia O'Keeffe, Diego Rivera, Mary Cassatt, and Edward Hopper, among others.

Location:

6000 N. New Braunfels Ave. San Antonio, TX 78247, USA

Pass/Permit/Fees:

Admission is free on Sundays but charges $10 for adults and $5 for children.

Best Time to Visit:

The best time to visit this museum is from May to October, as the weather is usually great during these months. From November to April, you should visit the museum during the late evening or early morning hours.

How to Get There:

Take I-35 north or south towards downtown San Antonio, Texas. Take exit #240A for Cesar Chavez Blvd toward Market /North Alamo Street (US-281 North/I-35 North). Continue on N New Braunfels Ave, which is at the end of the off-ramp turn on the right side of the highway.

GPS Coordinates:

29.485776°N 98.456233°W

Nearest City or Town:

Aside from San Antonio, the closest city is New Braunfels, which is approximately 15 miles north of this museum location.

Did You Know:

The McNay Art Museum is a member of the North American Reciprocal Museums Program and is one of only two private museums in the United States to be accredited by this organization.

93. CAMANCHE LOOKOUT PARK

Why You Should Visit:

Camanche Lookout Park is a great place to visit if you have a love for water, wildlife, and nature. Most of this park is surrounded by the Camanche Reservoir, so visitors will see many types of birds and other animals while visiting here. There is only one public boat ramp on the reservoir, which is located in the southwestern corner of the park. The park also contains a swimming beach with sandy shores and concession stands providing drinks and snacks.

Location:

15551 Nacogdoches Rd, San Antonio, TX 78247, USA

Pass/Permit/Fees:

Admission is $2 for adults with proof of age. Free admission is offered to Hays County, Texas, residents or visitors staying in San Antonio.

Best Time to Visit:

The best time to visit this park is in April-December, as it's warmer outside during these months.

How to Get There:

Take Loop 410 (access road) toward San Antonio, TX. On the left side of the 4-lane highway, take exit #22A for Interstate 35 / Loop 410 toward Austin and Exit 5B for McAllister Freeway (I-35 South). Continue onto Loop 410 East (signs for I-35 S/I-410 E/US 90 E/US 190 E). Take exit #5 for NW Military Hwy / US 90 (exit 5B). Merge onto NW Military Hwy/US 90 W. Turn left onto Nacogdoches Rd. The park will be on your right-hand side.

GPS Coordinates:

29° 35' 4.5276" N and 98° 22' 3.7992" W

Nearest City or Town:

Aside from San Antonio, the closest city is Seguin, which is approximately 90 miles northwest of this park location.

Did You Know:

In June of 1975, the St. Louis Waterway Development Corporation donated most of the land to Camanche Reservoir Park Association. Then in 1976, Congressman Tom Loeffler and State Representative William Wingo discussed having the reservoir developed into a park along the shores of the Camanche Reservoir.

94. PEARL BREWERY

Why You Should Visit:

If you enjoy beer and history, then the Pearl Brewery is a must-visit! One of the oldest operating brewing operations in Texas, this company was founded in 1873. The brewery has two indoor tours that visitors can take. Tours are free, but reservations are recommended on the weekends. This brewery is located on Front Street and contains a museum, gift shop, and theater/concert venue called "the Pearl." The theater shows several movies yearly, from traveling filmmakers such as Godzilla to classic Disney films.

Location:

303 Pearl Pkwy, Suite 300, San Antonio, TX 78215, USA

Pass/Permit/Fees:

$3 Monday through Thursday and $8 Friday, Saturday, and Sunday.

Best Time to Visit:

The best time to visit this brewery is during May-September as it is cooler outside during these months, and other people will also visit the brewery.

How to Get There:

Take I-10 west towards downtown San Antonio. Exit at Cesar Chavez Drive/exit #238 and turn left onto Cesar Chavez Dr. Turn right onto N Presa St, and then turn right onto S Alamo Street. The brewery will be on the right-hand side across the street from Hemisfair Park.

GPS Coordinates:

29° 26' 38.69" N, -98° 28' 49.12" W

Nearest City or Town:

Aside from San Antonio, the closest city is King William, which is approximately 20 miles north of this brewery location.

Did You Know:

The Pearl Brewery opened in 1881 and was one of the first breweries to produce beer in Texas. It closed in 1976 after Prohibition had ended. Thomas Haas purchased it and reopened it in 1982 with a new concept called "Pearl Brewery." This business attracts over 250,000 visitors each year!

95. MARKET SQUARE (EL MERCADO)

Why You Should Visit:

If you love shopping and wandering around, then Market Square is a beautiful place to spend your time. It is a three-block outdoor plaza lined with shops and restaurants. The shops offer a wide range of handmade Mexican items, art, jewelry, and more. Market Square is located on Commerce Street between Houston and Dolorosa streets.

Location:

514 W Commerce St, San Antonio, TX 78207, USA

Pass/Permit/Fees:

Admission is free, but parking is available for $1.50 per hour with a 2-hour limit.

Best Time to Visit:

The best time to visit Market Square is anytime during the warmer months of April-October, as you can enjoy sitting at the tables outside and buying a variety of souvenirs.

How to Get There:

Take I-35 southbound, which will take you across the San Antonio River. Turn left onto Nacogdoches at the San Antonio River Bridge. Follow Nacogdoches to West Commerce Street, which will lead you to Market Square.

GPS Coordinates:

29° 25' 31.4328" N, 98° 29' 57.9768" W

Nearest City or Town:

Aside from San Antonio, the closest city is San Marcos, which is approximately 6 miles southwest of this location.

Did You Know:

Market Square was created in 1988 with funds from the City. It cost $1 million to create the Market Square, and it took two years to complete the project. The market was originally supposed to be a place for farmers and ranchers to sell their products.

96. SAN ANTONIO RIVER WALK

Source: Phil Slattery

Why You Should Visit:

Also known as Paseo del Rio, this area is a must-visit during your visit to San Antonio. This walkway was originally designed as an irrigation canal by the Spanish in the 1690s and later served as a riverfront promenade in 1888 by business owners. River Walk is on the National Register of Historic Places and has been in several TV shows, like The Brady Bunch, Gunsmoke, and Walker, Texas Ranger. Although the area primarily serves tourism today, it also includes historical buildings, restaurants, and hotels. Tour boats are available for visitors who want to explore the river further or want to take a cruise past downtown San Antonio landmarks.

Location:

849 E Commerce St, San Antonio, TX 78205, United States

Pass/Permit/Fees:

Free

Best Time to Visit:

It is ideal for visiting at night as the area is filled with lights, and it is a great opportunity to take pictures of the San Antonio skyline with the Riverwalk in the background. However, if you wish to enjoy walking along the Riverwalk, then visit during the day when it is less crowded.

How to Get There:

Take I-35 northbound, which will bring you to downtown San Antonio. Once downtown, take E Commerce Street northbound, which will lead you directly to the Riverwalk.

GPS Coordinates:

29.4229° N, 98.4847° W

Nearest City or Town:

Aside from San Antonio, the closest city is Laredo, which is approximately 130 miles east of this location.

Did You Know:
River Walk serves as a transportation route for the city of San Antonio, which makes it an important part of the city. The city of San Antonio has many bridges along River Walk, and tourists heavily use the area.

97. SAN ANTONIO MISSION NATIONAL HISTORICAL PARK

Why You Should Visit:

This historic mission in downtown San Antonio is a must-visit for many people. It was established in 1718 by Spanish priests and served as one of the oldest standing churches in Texas. The mission church is open to visitors, and tourists can climb to the top of the tower, where they will have a great view of San Antonio's famous Alamo Plaza. The mission also offers tours, Spanish music, concerts, and events throughout the year. So if you are a history buff, this is an ideal place to visit. It also contains many original artifacts from its origins, including furniture and clothing that were used in the mission at one time.

Location:

6701 San Jose Dr, San Antonio, Texas 78214, USA

Pass/Permit/Fees:

Free; however, donations are accepted.

Best Time to Visit:

The best time to visit this historic mission is spring, summer, and fall. The area is open during the week and on weekends with limited hours, so availability may be limited at times.

How to Get There:

Take I-10 Westbound, which will take you to Mexico Avenue Exit. Once off the exit, turn left onto San Jose Drive and travel toward downtown San Antonio for approximately .6 miles until you reach Mission Espada State Historic Site on your left.

GPS Coordinates:

29.3165° N, 98.4459° W

Nearest City or Town:

Aside from San Antonio, the closest city is Alamo Heights, which is approximately 7 miles south of this location.

Did You Know:

San Antonio Mission National Historical Park is one of the more popular attractions in San Antonio, with more than 50,000 annual visitors. The park has a gift shop where visitors can browse for souvenirs and books about mission history.

98. TOWER OF AMERICAS

Why You Should Visit:

Tower of Americas, located in San Antonio, is a 42-story tall observation tower that was completed in 1998 and is the biggest of its kind in the US. It offers visitors great views of the city and is a popular spot for visitors to take pictures. If you want to do something fun, you can also go to the tower at night and watch the lights of the city from up high. The tower offers fireworks, laser shows, and a variety of concerts throughout the year. If you are up for an adventure, you can also go up to the top observation deck, which offers panoramic views of San Antonio.

Location:

739 Tower of the Americas Way, San Antonio, TX 78205, USA

Pass/Permit/Fees:

$16.50 for adults; free for children ages 3 and under; $13 for seniors and those in the military; $12.00 for children 4 - 12.

Best Time to Visit:

To view the best views of the city, visit during the day.

How to Get There:

From I-37, take exit 232B and turn onto S Alamo St. Travel southbound on S Alamo St for approximately 2 miles until you reach Cesar Chavez Blvd (US 281). Turn left onto Cesar Chavez Blvd and continue traveling eastbound for .3 miles until you reach Tower of Americas Way on your left.

GPS Coordinates:

29.4190° N, 98.4836° W

Nearest City or Town:

Aside from San Antonio, the closest city is Balcones Heights, which is approximately 6 miles west of this location.

Did You Know:

The Tower of Americas was constructed next to the former site of the Alamo and is the second tallest structure in San Antonio.

99. EATON HILL NATURE CENTER & PRESERVE

Why You Should Visit:

Eaton Hill is a preserve located in the East Central region of Central Texas. The preserve contains rolling hills, beautiful oak trees, and a variety of animals, snakes, and other wild creatures. The preserve is home to many different species and can accommodate a wide variety of hikes. There are also picnic areas within the preserve for visitors who wish to bring their families and enjoy nature's beauty. Eaton Hill is one of the top places to visit in Texas if you are a bird enthusiast.

Location:

500 Cityhill Rd, Sonora, TX 76950, USA

Pass/Permit/Fees:

Trails are free of charge.

Best Time to Visit:

The best time to visit Eaton Hill Nature Preserve is spring, summer, and fall. However, in the fall, cool breezes usually make for a great hiking experience as well.

How to Get There:

From the intersection of US 287 and FM 855, go south on US 287 for approximately 4 miles. Turn right onto CR 250 and go west for 5 miles. The preserve's entrance will be located on the left side of the road.

GPS Coordinates:

30.0831° N, 99.6491° W

Nearest City or Town:

Aside from Sonora, the closest city is Cotulla, which is approximately 16.3 miles southeast of this location.

Did You Know:

The preserve is located on top of a dormant volcano, which makes for great soil and ideal surroundings for the animals and plants that reside in the preserve.

100. CAVERNS OF SONORA

Why You Should Visit:

Caverns of Sonora is a cave system located in the hill country of Central Texas. The caverns are very deep and contain many tunnels and underground lakes. The cave has become an attraction for travelers and locals alike because it is one of the few remaining natural caves on earth. Although most parts of the cave are closed to the public, a small entrance inside the Aquarium at SeaWorld can be visited during certain hours. There are also some short hiking trails that lead to different parts of the cavern system.

Location:

1711 Private Rd 4468, Sonora, TX 76950, USA

Pass/Permit/Fees:

The admission costs $20 per person, including a tour that lasts approximately 1 hour and 15 minutes.

Best Time to Visit:

The months from July through September are the best time to visit as more daylight hours are available. However, it is best to plan a visit before the summer season begins so that you can have more time to explore the caverns.

How to Get There:

From the intersection of US 287 and FM 855, go south on US 287 for approximately 4 miles. Turn right onto CR 250 and go west for 5 miles.

GPS Coordinates:

30.555°N, 100.81227°W

Nearest City or Town:

Aside from Sonora, the next closest city to the Caverns of Sonora is Kerrville, which is approximately 45.3 miles north of this location.

Did You Know:

The caverns of Sonora contain a high level of calcite, which has made them last longer than most other natural caves.

101. KRAUSE SPRINGS

Source: Larry D. Moore

Why You Should Visit:

It is a popular spring site for visitors because of the crystal clear springs and the caves surrounding it. Krause Springs offers visitors great views and a variety of activities that include canoeing, swimming, hiking, camping, and picnicking.

Location:

424 Co Rd 404, Spicewood, TX 78669, United States

Pass/Permit/Fees:

$6 per person with a maximum of 128 people. $2 to enter the park.

Best Time to Visit:

The water in the spring is usually at its coolest temperature between December and June, and it gets warmer as you get closer to the end of January.

How to Get There:

From I-35, take exit 44 and go south for approximately 1 mile until you reach Co Rd 404 (which runs east-west) on the left. Turn left onto Co Rd 404 and go east for 2 miles. The park can be found on your right side at the intersection of Co Rd 123. The campground will be located on your left just before you reach the park entrance.

GPS Coordinates:

30°28'39.7"N 98°9'6.0"W

Nearest City or Town:

Aside from Spicewood, the next closest city is Austin, which is approximately 52.6 miles west of this location.

Did You Know:

The water in the springs comes from two different sources. One of the sources is the Edwards limestone, and the other source is a natural aquifer.

102. PACE BEND PARK

Why You Should Visit:
With more than 9 miles of Lake Travis shoreline, it is one of the most popular areas in the Highland Lakes region, offering a variety of recreational opportunities. The park's west side is characterized by high limestone cliffs and numerous rocky coves that provide some of the most breathtaking views of Lake Travis, especially at sunset. On the east side, the park includes a wide undeveloped beach with huge sand dunes that overlook the clear waters of Lake Travis.

Location:
2805 Pace Bend Rd N, Spicewood, TX 78669, USA

Pass/Permit/Fees:
A $3 fee per vehicle is required. Season passes for Pace Bend Park can be purchased for $30.

Best Time to Visit:
The best time to visit this park is between January and March when light rain and cold temperatures provide a perfect environment for the lakefront.

How to Get There:
From the intersection of US 183 and RM 620, go east on RM 620 for approximately 9 miles, where you will reach Pace Bend Park on your right side. The entrance will be just before you reach Lake Travis.

GPS Coordinates:
30.4596° N, 98.0192° W

Nearest City or Town:
Aside from Spicewood, the next closest city to Pace Bend Park is Austin, which is approximately 54.0 miles west of this location.

Did You Know:
The park offers visitors recreational opportunities, including picnicking, hiking, swimming, biking/mountain biking, and paddle boats.

103. SUGAR LAND TOWN SQUARE

Source: Ed Schipul

Why You Should Visit:
Sugar Land Town Square is the most recognizable downtown in Sugar Land and is one of the most visited tourist attractions within Sugar Land. The Sugar Land Town Square offers visitors a wide variety of shopping, dining, and entertainment locations, as well as many historical sites and monuments. The Sugar Land Town Square also serves as the central location for most of the city's special events and community celebrations.

Location:
15958 City Walk, Sugar Land, TX 77479, USA

Pass/Permit/Fees:
No fee.

Best Time to Visit:
The best time to visit the Sugar Land Town Square is during the Christmas holidays when there are several holiday activities and events that take place in this popular tourist attraction as well as during the Easter season when the Town Square becomes home to a number of colorful egg hunts and crafts.

How to Get There:
Sugar Land Town Square is located on the north side of I-45. From the intersection of Town and County Roads, go east on Town Road for approximately 1 mile, where you will cross over I-45 to reach the south side of I-45. Sugar Land Town Square is located on your left at the corner of Town and County Roads.

GPS Coordinates:
29.5960° N, 95.6218° W

Nearest City or Town:
Aside from Sugar Land, the next closest city is Houston, which is approximately 96.0 miles west of this location.

Did You Know:
The Sugar Land Town Square is home to the largest life-size nativity scene in the United States, which continues to be a popular tourist attraction during the Christmas season.

104. FAR FLUNG OUTDOOR CENTER

Why You Should Visit:

The Far Flung Outdoor Center has everything that you need for a fun-filled weekend of camping and enjoying the great outdoors. The facility includes a campground with over 170 total campsites, tent sites, and RV campsites with water and electric hookups. It also offers visitors a number of recreational opportunities, including swimming, kayaking, canoeing, boating, and fishing, as well as a 9-hole golf course.

Location:

23310 FM170, Terlingua, TX 79852, USA

Pass/Permit/Fees:

Far Flung Outdoor Center membership plans are offered for a low price. The first month's service fee is free. Membership fees begin at $30 for an individual and $90 for an individual plus a household unit. Individuals who have been members for at least six months may pay no more than what they paid the previous year.

Best Time to Visit:

The best time to visit the Far Flung Outdoor Center is between December and May when the weather is mild and ideal for outdoor activities.

How to Get There:

From SH 170 (the main route into this part of Terlingua), go east for approximately 4 miles until you reach the Far Flung Outdoor Center on your left. The facility will be located just across from the Terlingua Ranch Resort.

GPS Coordinates:

29.5770° N, 103.9796° W

Nearest City or Town:

Aside from Terlingua, the next closest city is Sanderson, which is approximately 26.5 miles southeast of this location.

Did You Know:

The Far Flung Outdoor Center was founded in 1978 and has been a popular tourist attraction ever since.

105. BIG BEND NATIONAL PARK

Why You Should Visit:
With nearly 5 million acres of rugged mountain terrain, desert landscapes, and wide open expanses of desert grassland, Big Bend National Park offers visitors various recreational activities, including hiking, camping, and sightseeing. Additionally, the park is home to several endangered species, including bighorn sheep and greater roadrunners.

Location:
Barton Warnock, 21800 FM 170, Terlingua, TX 79852, USA

Pass/Permit/Fees:
The entrance fee is $30 per vehicle or $15 per person (both valid for seven days) unless you have a parking pass.

Best Times to Visit:
The ideal time to visit is between March and November when temperatures are neither too hot nor too cold, there is typically little precipitation, and summer has not yet begun.

How to Get There:
From US 385 (the main route into this part of Terlingua), go east for approximately 12 miles until you reach the park entrance on your right. Bear left onto US 385 and go north for 22 miles, where you will reach the park entrance and parking lot on your left.

GPS Coordinates:
29.269902° N, -103.757351° W

Nearest City or Town:
Aside from Terlingua, the next closest city is Alpine, which is approximately 31.8 miles southeast of this location.

Did You Know:
Fossils of prehistoric creatures and mammoths have been found in Big Bend National Park and are on permanent display at the park's Visitor Center. The park also offers educational programs, guided tours for school groups, and outreach programs that allow students to participate in hands-on activities with real-life scientists.

106. LONE STAR MOTORCYCLE MUSEUM AND HALL OF FAME

Why You Should Visit:

The Lone Star Motorcycle Museum and Hall of Fame is home to the largest motorcycle collection in the world, with over 250 vintage and modern motorcycles located in its 25,000-square-foot building. Suppose you are in the mood for a good old-fashioned motorcycle trip. In that case, the Lone Star Museum has everything you need, including leather jackets with a backpack and saddlebags, helmets with visors and radios, hand-tooled boots, and leather gloves. The museum also maintains an extensive collection of other rare and vintage motorcycles from around the world as well as military vehicles used by the United States military during times of war.

Location:

36517 RM 187, Vanderpool, TX 78885, USA

Pass/Permit/Fees:

Admission for kids 15 and under is free; $7 for 16 and above.

Best Times to Visit:

The crowd of motorcycle enthusiasts increases in this location during the summer months of June, July, and August, when the weather is ideal for riding motorcycles.

How to Get There:

From SH 176 (the main route into this part of Terlingua), go north for approximately 7 miles until you reach Vanderpool on your left. Continue north for approximately 2 miles until you reach the motel located on your right. Continue north for another 2 miles from here until you reach the Lone Star Motorcycle Museum and Hall of Fame on your right.

GPS Coordinates:

28.923096° N, -103.765943° W

Nearest City or Town:

Aside from Terlingua, the next closest city is El Paso, which is approximately 126 miles southwest of this location.

Did You Know:

The collection of vintage motorcycles at the Lone Star Motorcycle Museum and Hall of Fame has won a number of awards over the years for its large assortment and high quality. It was also named to "Motorcycle Consumer News" 10 Best List for 2014-2016!

107. LOST MAPLES STATE NATURAL AREA

Source: Larry D. Moore

Why You Should Visit:

The park contains beautiful scenery, wildlife, and plant life native to the region and is, therefore, a great place to visit if you wish to see nature in Texas at its finest. The redwoods of Lost Maples contain more than beauty–they also contain many different species of plants and animals. Many visitors also enjoy hiking, bird watching, horseback riding on trails that are open to horses, biking, and photography.

Location:

37221 RM 187, Vanderpool, TX 78885, USA

Pass/Permit/Fees:

There is no entrance fee, but there are a number of camping and recreational fees.

Best Time to Visit:

The fall, around the months of September and October, is when the weather is best for outdoor activities throughout Lost Maples State Natural Area.

How to Get There:

From US 87, go south for about 13 miles until you reach San Saba. Turn left onto RR 187 for about 1.7 miles. You'll see the entrance to the park on your right.

GPS Coordinates:

29°49'11"N, 99°34'59"W

Nearest City or Town:

Aside from Vanderpool, the next closest city is San Saba, which is approximately 12 miles northeast of this location.

Did You Know:

Trees were once thought to only grow in full sun and fertile soil, but it was later discovered that trees are not born with these qualities in their genes. Therefore, trees can be successfully grown elsewhere and then transplanted to a spot where they can develop into full-grown trees. Lost Maples is one of the many places where this operation occurs.

108. MAGNOLIA MARKET AT THE SILOS

Why You Should Visit:

If you are a fan of the popular HGTV show "Fixer Upper," you will want to pay a visit to the Magnolia Market at the Silos. The Silos are home to two shops, the Hearth & Hand store (which sells many items from Fixer Upper) and the Magnolia Market (which sells all things Chip and Joanna Gaines). These shops are filled with items for decorating and completing your home in a beautiful and unique way. You can also attend events held here throughout the year, including vendor fairs, special appearances by Chip and Joanna, concerts, and holiday celebrations.

Location:

601 Webster Ave, Waco, TX 76706, United States

Pass/Permit/Fees:

There is no entrance fee to this location.

Best Time to Visit:

Fall and winter are the best times to go to Magnolia Market at the Silos because the weather is good for shopping.

How to Get There:

From I-35, exit 215 (Waco), and head north on the main road. Take a left at the light (Briarwood Forest Boulevard), heading east until you reach Webster Avenue. Turn right and drive until you reach Magnolia Market at the Silos on your left.

GPS Coordinates:

31.5526° N, 97.1294° W

Nearest City or Town:

Aside from Waco, the next closest city is Dallas, which is approximately 35 miles southeast of this location.

Did You Know:

Once upon a time, Waco was known as the "Queen City of Texas." That title changed during the Civil War because of Union troops who captured the city and burned all of its buildings, leaving only Magnolia Market at the Silos standing.

109. JACOB'S WELL

Source: Larry D. Moore

Why You Should Visit:

Jacob's Well is a natural spring that has been the location of many stories and legends. Nestled in a beautiful valley surrounded by hills, Jacob's Well is perfect for pleasure or relaxation any time of the day. It has been said that the water of Jacob's Well has healing powers, and throughout its history, people have traveled far and wide to see the well for themselves. The water in the well is crystal clear due to the fact that it is filled with sand, gravel, and limestone. Despite its long history, Jacob's Well has become increasingly popular in recent years because of social media posts.

Location:

1699 Mt Sharp Rd, Wimberley, TX 78676, USA

Pass/Permit/Fees:

Admission is free. You may swim in the well, but you must be careful because there are no lifeguards on duty.

Best Time to Visit:

The months of July and August are the best months to visit Jacob's Well because the weather is most suitable for swimming.

How to Get There:

From US 281 north of Wimberley, exit at E. 1612 Road. Follow this road until it intersects with Hwy 16 West (FM 2127). From here, follow the signs for Jacob's Well and Old Highway 27.

GPS Coordinates:

30° 2.1129' N, 98° 7.0696.' W

Nearest City or Town:

Aside from Wimberley, the next closest city is Austin, which is approximately 50 miles to the east of this location.

Did You Know:

Jacob's Well is the only natural Texas spring with no fish.

110. BOYKIN SPRINGS RECREATION AREA

Why You Should Visit:

Boykin Springs Recreation Area is a large park, suitable for all ages, that offers plenty of recreational opportunities and beautiful scenery. Most people who visit this area come to go swimming in the pool and enjoy the stunning view of the Colorado River. You can also enjoy a picnic beneath beautiful trees or play on playgrounds that are specifically designed for young children. If you are feeling energetic, you can check out the fitness trails located throughout the park or try your luck at fishing along the river banks.

Location:

Forest Service Rd 313, Zavalla, TX 75980, USA

Pass/Permit/Fees:

To use the pool, you must be a Texas resident, but anyone can go fishing. Day passes are available for those who are not residents of Texas.

Best Time to Visit:

The best time of year to visit Boykin Springs Recreation Area is during the summer months when the weather is most suitable for swimming and fishing, but you can enjoy this location all year round, depending on what you plan on doing while you are here.

How to Get There:

From Hwy 75, take FM 680 (Forest Service Road 313) southwest of Zavalla.

GPS Coordinates:

32° 7.3008' N, 94° 9.3689' W

Nearest Town or City:

Aside from Zavalla, the closest city is Jacksboro, which is approximately 10 miles south of Boykin Springs Recreation Area.

Did You Know:

The pool at Boykin Springs Recreation Area was the site of the first hot tub in Texas.

THE PRIMEVELER TEXAS TRIPS PROPOSAL

1. THE BEST WAY TO DISCOVER TEXAS WEEK ITINERARY

This week is called "the best way to discover Texas" because it combines all the best things to do in Texas. From discovering the history of Texas in San Antonio, going for seafood at Galveston, seeing an incredible view of Texas on your way to Dallas, or lying under a blanket watching one of the many music festivals around Austin and Houston. If you want, you can add more days by visiting some other cities like Dallas or San Antonio, where you can get more done.

Day 1: Austin

The ideal place to start your trip is in Austin. There are a number of sights you can visit if you have the time, including museums and tours. First, you should visit the Texas Capitol building on the grounds of the Capitol complex. It houses many interesting exhibits that are worth an hour or two of your time. The next stop is Mount Bonnell and Pennybacker Bridge. Mount Bonnell is a hill that you can hike to the top from downtown Austin. Pennybacker Bridge is a suspension bridge that spans Lady Bird Lake, the largest natural lake in Texas. The bridge was built in 1914 and underwent several renovations to make it more modern in 1949, but for its innovative design. You can take a boat cruise on Lady Bird Lake or visit Barton Springs Pool at sunset if you have time. The locals recommend going to the Boardwalk at Lady Bird Lake at night. The Boardwalk is a pedestrian walk along the banks of Lady Bird Lake with restaurants and shopping places, so it's very lively in the evenings. You can eat pizza and drink beer along the water's edge or visit a local music club where great live bands perform late into the night.

Day 2: Explore Austin

The next day you can further explore Austin. The best place to start is the Bullock Texas State History Museum. It's a very large museum, so you'll need at least a day to visit all the exhibits. Some of the highlights are the tram tour that takes you on a ride through the history of Texas, from before the Spanish arrival in 1690 and up to modern times with President George W. Bush, former governor of Texas. The museum also offers many temporary exhibits, so check their website for updates. After visiting the museum, go for lunch and a visit to the mall. Some of the best places to eat are Italian Pizzeria, Sushi House, great Italian food that is really good and very cheap, or I Love Taste Mexican Grill. This restaurant serves tasty Mexican specialties with an extensive margarita menu. You can also check out one of the new bars and pubs on 6th Street, such as The Blackheart Bar. Great live music in a laid-back atmosphere but still in the heart of Austin's entertainment district. Many other great bars and pubs can be found along 6th Street if you want to explore Austin's nightlife scene further.

Day 3: Day Trip to San Antonio

San Antonio is less than two hours away and one of the best Texas cities to visit, so plan a day trip there on your third day. The Market Square (El Mercado) in San Antonio's Lower Downtown is an excellent starting point. The Market Square is a popular tourist spot with many interesting shops and restaurants that you can explore while you eat your lunch. After lunch, plan to visit Pearl Brewery Historic District, which was the city's first brewery in America. The buildings and the surroundings are magnificent; it has been designated a National Historic Landmark. Afterward, at night visit the

Riverwalk. The Riverwalk is a riverfront area in downtown San Antonio that is always packed with people, especially in the evenings. It's a great spot to go out and experience San Antonio's nightlife scene.

Day 4: Houston

Houston is just over two hours away from Austin and a great city to visit. So plan a day trip there on your fourth day. A good place to start is Sam Houston Park, which is home to the site of Sam Houston's grave, one of the most important figures in Texas history and the founder of Houston. After you visit the park, go for a walk along Battleship Texas, an old battleship that was converted into a museum. Take a tour of the exhibits, or explore them on your own. Eat your lunch downtown and visit the Space Center Houston, one of the largest science centers in the world. There you can check out the exhibits on space, with a mess of rockets and other things, or visit the Space Center gift shop and buy some postcards that are very geeky!

Day 5: Houston to Galveston

Spend your last day in Texas exploring the beaches at Galveston. It is less than one hour away from Houston and is a perfect place to chill out. In close proximity to the 61st Street Fishing Pier in Galveston, one of the best fishing piers in the United States, are numerous restaurants, bars, and shops. If you have the time, head to The Seawall to watch the sunset over the Gulf of Mexico or dine at a beachfront restaurant. Afterward, go back to The Strand, the city's famous historic district, where you can visit many shops and restaurants. You should try out The Galveston Island Historic Pleasure Pier. It is a great amusement park built on a pier that stretches over the Gulf of Mexico!

Day 6: To Dallas

Drive to Dallas on your last day; it's less than two hours away from Galveston. When you get there, head straight to the Southside area to visit Dealey Plaza, where JFK was shot; then go to the Sixth Floor Museum at Dealey Plaza to learn more about the event. Afterward, go to Bishop Arts District for some great restaurants and shopping. You can eat at one of the many restaurants, have a glass of wine at one of the many wine bars, or go shopping for some cool stuff for your friends and family back home. If you have time, go to Reunion Tower, the tallest structure in Texas, and watch the sunset over the city, or you can eat your dinner at one of the observatory restaurants at the top.

Day 7: Travel Home

Now it's time to pack up your bags and head home. Don't forget to buy some souvenirs!

This itinerary is more about relaxation and enjoying the scenery while learning the history of Texas. It is more of a slow-paced tour, so it is not recommended for those who want to travel around and party every night. Nothing is wrong with partying, but remember to have fun in a more laid-back style!

2. KNOWING TEXAS WEEK ITINERARY

You can call this trip "Knowing Texas"—this is basically what you achieve after going through all these great places. If you follow this itinerary and do not get distracted, you will definitely know the state of Texas in detail after going through all the historical events and attractions. This trip is great for people who love history because they will learn much about Texas and its past.

Day 1: Fort Worth

Fort Worth is a quaint and quiet city with a nice nightlife scene. It can be a great way to start your week here. You start the day early to can see some of the city's best. Start at Fort Worth Botanic Garden in the morning. Spend some time here, and learn about the plants and trees. Afterward, go to Fort Worth Nature Center & Refuge, the largest wildlife refuge in Texas. You can check out the wildlife and see a lot of different animals, which is a nice way to learn about Texas. When you are done, go to the Fort Worth Zoo and check out all the animals there. Afterward, head to The Stockyards and watch some rodeos. You might even be able to try your hand at roping a calf! After being exhausted by all of that riding, galloping, heeling, bucking, and kicking, you'll end the day with a beer at The Railhead or Rodeo Diner for some good barbecue!

Day 2: Fort Worth to Amarillo

Amarillo is a small town with a rich history. Fort Worth is less than two hours away, but that does not mean you should hurry there. Spend the day getting to know Amarillo. Start at Palo Duro Canyon State Park, home to some of the most amazing rock formations in the United States, including the "pothole" caves formed by hot springs millions of years ago. It's one of the unique things to do in Texas. Check out the hiking trails; there are some really stunning views of Texas from up there. Afterward, go to Cadillac Ranch, a great roadside attraction with 10 Cadillacs buried nose-first in the ground. It is one of the best activities in Texas, so you should not miss it. After that, drive around town and explore Amarillo. Go to local favorites like The Live Stock Exchange, and finish your day with dinner at The Feedlot!

Day 3: Amarillo to El Paso

El Paso is in the southwest of Texas, so it makes sense to head there on your third day. The drive from Amarillo is only about 3 hours. Spend the first part of your day at Chamizal National Memorial, which is located on the U.S.-Mexico border. Check out the visitor center that shows how the U.S.-Mexico border was moved in the past, and walk around the park to see some of the monuments that were built to commemorate those events. Afterward, head to Old Fort Bliss Replica and Fort Bliss History Museum. They are worth seeing, so don't miss this opportunity.

If you still have time, go to Hueco Tanks State Historic Site, one of the most historically diverse sites in Texas. It is located in the Chihuahuan Desert, and many trails will guide you through it. You can see some of the most beautiful rock art and learn about some really interesting history here. After all this history, go back to El Paso and finish the day with a margarita at a local restaurant!

Day 4: El Paso to Fredericksburg

Fredericksburg is a small town, but it has so much to offer. As it is a 7-hour drive from El Paso, start at Wildseed Farms and wander around their vineyards. You will find some really delicious wine and food here, and you can relax in the quiet atmosphere here. Afterward, go to the Enchanted Rock State

Natural Area. This is a beautiful place with lots of hiking trails and rock formations. The views are great, and the park itself is really enjoyable to explore. You can watch the sunset from here as well. After all, this tiring activity, head to your hotel and relax for the night!

Day 5: Explore Fredericksburg

Fredericksburg is a great place to visit because it has so many things to do. Start your day by heading to Pioneer Museum. This place gives you some insight into the lives of the frontiersmen who settled in Texas. It is a great experience to learn about their lives. After wandering through these historical items, explore the town of Fredericksburg and find some great places to eat! Fredericksburg has some of the best BBQ and wine (if you did not try this out while you were in Wildseed Farms), so be sure to try that. If you are a shopper, this is also a great place because there are many antique shops here. After you are done, head to Fort Martin Scott and learn about the historical events that took place there. You can also go here to see the beautiful view of Texas.

If you still have time, go to Willow City Loop, a historic town with a beautiful church, cafe, and many other interesting things to see. You can take in the beauty of Texas from the top of the hill and learn some more great history as well. Finally, head to the Fredericksburg Music Hall if you want to go out. This place is a great place to see some local music, such as bluegrass, country, and rock. You will have a chance to see some really cool shows there!

Day 6: Fredericksburg to Amarillo

Amarillo is a great place to end your trip because it is located in the center of the state. It is an expansive city with so much going on it. Get in the car and get ready for an exciting day of driving! Start at Henley-Denny Ranch State Historical Park. When you get there, take in all the amazing scenery surrounding this area.

Day 6: Fredericksburg to Corpus Christi

Corpus Christi is located on the Gulf Coast, so you can enjoy all the beaches there. The trip from Fredericksburg to Corpus Christi is about 3 hours, so get in the car and head out! Check out Corpus Christi Downtown Seawall at the beginning of your trip. This area is full of vibrant colors and great people. Take a walk down the Seawall and see all of the great sights there. After that, go to the South Texas Music Walk of Fame and see some of the artists who were inducted into this place. You can get some free souvenirs and learn about great musicians who shaped the music industry. After all of this walking, go to one of the local restaurants to enjoy a delicious meal!

If you still have time, visit the Watergardens Fountains, which are located at Corpus Christi Beach. This fountain park has a huge garden and many beautiful fountains. It is a wonderful location for strolling and viewing the vibrant colors of Texas.

Day 7: Prepare to Go Home

After all the fun you had in Texas, it is time to head home. Prepare for the long drive back to your home, and go through all of the great things you saw during your trip. If you could visit everything on the itinerary, this was the best trip you have ever taken!

This itinerary is more on learning the history of Texas while doing a bit of sightseeing. It is a great road trip for people who want to learn about the state's history and enjoy some great activities!

Travel
JOURNAL SECTION

Date of Visit: _____   Number of Days Spent: _____

WEATHER CONDITIONS

WHAT I VISITED

WHAT I BOUGHT

WHERE I SLEPT

WHERE I ATE

WHO I MET

SECTION TO MARK THE SCORE FROM 0 TO 10

0   1   2   3   4   5   6   7   8   9   10

THE MOST BEAUTIFUL MEMORY

DOWNLOAD YOUR PACKING CHECKLIST HERE!

Made in the USA
Coppell, TX
27 March 2023

14792355R00090